IDEAS FOR LIVING

Ideas for

Living

ERNEST HOLMES

Compiled and Edited by
WILLIS KINNEAR

SCIENCE OF MIND PUBLICATIONS
Los Angeles, California

First Printing — June 1972

Published by SCIENCE OF MIND PUBLICATIONS
3251 West Sixth Street, Los Angeles, California 90075

ISBN 0-911336-40-0

CONTENTS

FOREWORD

There comes a time in every man's life when he feels there needs to be something more added to his experience of living.

Just what is needed may not be known, so the only recourse is to explore a variety of ideas in the hope that one which may be found is the answer and provides a larger, more gratifying life.

The thoughts encountered in the pages of his volume are greatly diversified, but at the same time there seems to be a consistent basic philosophy: the universe is a great Unity, and man is Life's crowning achievement on Earth.

Man's greater awareness of his relationship to all that is opens the door of unlimited possibilities for him. One of the ideas for living you discover could be the start of a new way of life for you.

For this book there have been selected fifteen pertinent and inspiring ideas from the writings of Ernest Holmes. A few of these appeared in print many years ago and are no longer available; the rest are from the store of his unpublished material.

This is the sixteenth volume of Ernest Holmes' writings to appear since his passing on in 1960. For those new to his writings, he is known as one of the great metaphysical philosophers of our day. His outstanding work, *The Science of Mind,* is the classic in this field. He also established *Science of Mind* Magazine.

WILLIS KINNEAR
Director
Science of Mind Publications

8

INTRODUCTION

Man is a center of self-conscious life. Infinite Intelligence is the Life Principle animating man. While this Life Principle is forever hidden from our objective view, we are continuously conscious of Its existence in us and animating all nature. The relationship between the Life Principle and that which It sustains is self-evidently one of unity. The highest perception of mankind has been his sense of this inner oneness with the Spirit. The more completely we become conscious of this Divine union, the more power we have over our own existence. But we should not limit the unity of God with man to the religious field alone, for this has been one of the great mistakes of the ages.

We should not separate Life from living, Spirit from matter, nor Divine Principle from a universal creation. God is "all in all"; that is, God is, and is in everything. The gardener finds a Divine idea concealed in the seed; loosed into action this idea produces the plant. The geologist finds the imprints of invisible forces in the rock. The evolutionist reads the history of cosmic activities on this planet as he deciphers the unfolding of an intelligent Life Force carrying creatiion forward to its consummating point here, which is the production of self-conscious life. The scientist finds an energy concealed in the atom, and the spiritual genius discloses an intuitive knowledge which can be accounted for only on the theory that "we lie in the lap of an infinite intelligence."

So close is the union of creation with the Creator that it is impossible to say where one begins and the other leaves off. Emerson tells us that "Spirit is matter reduced to its extreme thinness," and Spinoza tells us that mind and matter are the same thing, while Jesus boldly proclaimed that the very words which he spoke were Spirit and were Life. Robert Browning tells us of a spark which a man may desecrate but never quite lose, and he further proclaims that we are all Gods, though in the germ. Wordsworth sensed that heaven is the native home of all mankind, and Tennyson said that more things are wrought by prayer than this world dreams. Shakespeare perceived sermons in stones and good in everything.

Science is on the verge of disclosing a spiritual Universe and will ultimately make the declaration that what we call the material universe is a spontaneous emergence, through evolution, of inner forces which cannot be explained but which must be accepted. How, then, can we doubt that the very mind which we use is some manifestation of that Intelligence which is in all that lives?

ERNEST HOLMES

CHAPTER I

MAN'S GREATEST DISCOVERY

The greatest discovery ever made is the discovery of the creative power of thought. Our thought can help us in healing our body and it can help us to control the circumstances and situations around us. But if we were to ask, How is thought creative? we could not answer this question any more than the question, Why does a chicken come out of an egg? or, Why do acorns become oak trees? or, Why does gravity hold everything in place? When we discover a principle in nature we have to accept it. No, we cannot explain why thought is creative, but we can and must accept the fact that it is and see what we can do with it.

Just as gravitational force operates on physical objects to hold them in place, so there is another kind of force that operates on our thinking and tends to bring into our experience those things which are dominant in our mind. This explains why faith is effective because faith is an affirmative attitude of mind that uses the creative power of thought constructively. It gives us a key to the teachings of Jesus about prayer.

We can use the laws of nature consciously and decide what we want them to do for us, but we are not these laws, they are greater than we are. We may have implicit confidence in them because we know they will never fail. We know that when we plant a certain kind of seed we will get a certain kind of plant. We know that when we mix certain colors together we will get another color. We do the planting and the mixing, but nature produces the results. If we can keep these simple thoughts in mind and come to realize that the creative power of our thought is a power that we take out of nature rather than put in, it will be a great help to us.

We are surrounded by a Law of Mind which acts on our thought. This is the security of our faith and the answer to prayer. It is flowing through us even as It flows around us. It is creative and operates in everything we do. This Principle is limitless in Its ability and can do anything we can conceive of Its doing and will do anything for us we can believe It will, providing we use It for good and constructive purposes.

But we have not quite accepted the idea that spiritual Law is just as real as physical law. Perhaps we think it is not right for us to use spiritual Law for personal purposes, and yet we use other laws in nature for personal purposes and there can be nothing wrong in using any law for any purpose that is constructive.

To Jesus spiritual Law was just as real as physical laws are to us. He knew that there is a silent, invisible, creative Force which acts on us and through us at all times, whether or not we believe it, and his purpose and mission in life was to show us that this Law exists, how It works, and how to use It in such a way that only good will result.

Jesus never said that it is wrong to be happy. He never intimated that God wishes us to be sick or poor or disconsolate. Quite the reverse. He used spiritual Power for every conceivable purpose, for what we call small things as well as big things. And he said that everything he did was an example for us to follow and that if we do, definite signs will follow our belief, our faith, and our acceptance.

If, then, we can come to see that such a Law exists and that we are using a Power greater than we are, we shall at once be relieved of any sense of responsibility, as though we had to make the Law work. For we do not sit around holding thoughts or trying to compel things to happen. As a matter of fact, this would defeat the very purpose we wish to accomplish. We can no more make the Law of Mind creative than we can compel an acorn to become an oak. We do not hold thoughts over the acorn nor do we visualize an oak tree. What we do is to plant an acorn and let nature create the oak tree for us.

This invisible Force was real to Jesus. He had implicit faith in It. And because he did, all those things which have seemed so miraculous followed. He was a spiritual scientist who had come to understand that there is a universal Principle of Mind, a creative Intelligence which acted on his faith and conviction. He could tell the paralyzed man to get up and walk, turn the water into wine, and multiply the loaves and fishes by a process which, to him, was just as natural as it would be for us to use any of the laws of nature with which we are familiar.

He used a Power which all people have, but which few people are aware of. And he plainly told his followers that they could do the same thing. Some of his immediate followers did experience the same miraculous signs following their belief. And throughout the ages these signs have followed many people's belief.

To understand that our faith is operated on by a natural law gives us the key to the situation. But it is not enough just to believe in a principle. This is only the starting point. Principles have to be used if they are going to produce definite results for us, and whether the principles are physical, mental, or spiritual makes no difference.

It is not enough to say that faith can do anything, for most people already believe this. What we have to do is not only to realize that faith *can* do things; we have to find out how faith is acquired and then we have to use it for definite purposes.

To merely state that we believe that God is all there is will not necessarily cause anything to happen. But when we believe that God is all there is, and when we have implicit confidence in the Law of Good, and when we use this belief for a definite purpose, then something will happen. And the reason why it happens is that we are surrounded by a creative Power, a creative Mind, or a creative Principle — whatever we choose to call It. We are surrounded by such a creative Power which actually does operate on our thinking. This is the key to the whole situation.

Let us, then, learn to make known our requests with thanksgiving and in acceptance. And having done this, in that silent communion of our soul with its Source, let us believe that the Law of Mind will do the rest.

Therefore, say to yourself, quietly and with deep conviction:

I now accept my Divine birthright. I now consciously enter into my partnership with Love, with Peace, with Joy, with God. I feel the infinite Presence close around me. I feel the warmth, the color, and the radiance of this Presence like a living thing in which I am enveloped.

I am no longer afraid of life. A deep and abiding sense of calm and poise flows through me. I have faith to believe that the Kingdom of God is at hand. It is right where I am, here, now, today, at this moment.

I feel that there is a Divine Law which can, will, and does govern everything. Therefore, I feel that everything in my thought that is life-giving, everything in my life that is constructive, is blessed and prospered. It blesses everyone I meet. It makes glad every situation in which I find myself. It brings peace and comfort to everyone I contact. I am united with everything in life, in love, in peace, and in joy. And I know that the Presence of Love and Life gently leads me and all others, guiding, guarding, sustaining, upholding — now and forever. And so it is.

CHAPTER II

EVERY MAN'S SEARCH

Every man's search is after something that will make him whole and happy, something that will cause him to feel safe and secure, and, I believe, something that will make him certain that he is going to live forever somewhere. We cannot believe that the Divine Intelligence which has created everything, including ourselves, could possibly have done this without at the same time providing a way through which we may live as happy and whole human beings, or Divine beings.

Jesus said that he was the way, the truth, and the life. He had discovered the secret which not only delivered all Life and Love to him, but at the same time it delivered all Power to him. It is this Life, this Love, and this Power that he came to tell us about. Since he so completely proved his point, it is wise for us to follow the rules he laid down for us. He stated one of these rules when he told us that we must lose our lives if we wish to find them.

At first this seems like a very hard and strange thing to do. For none of us really wishes to lose his life. It cannot be possible that Jesus meant that we should literally lose our lives, rather, that there must be things in our lives that we should let go of, as he said to the crippled woman: ". . . thou art loosed from thine infirmity." There must be something that is attached to us that does not really belong to the real man that Jesus was talking about. And so we should seek to find the fundamental truth that he taught.

If we do this we shall find that he laid the greatest emphasis on the idea that we are spiritual beings, living in a spiritual universe right now; that God, the supreme Spirit and Intelligence in the universe and the Power that governs everything, is not some far-off Presence, but something that is immediate, a Presence that is here with us now. Jesus said that this Presence is not only with us, It is within us; we live in It and It moves through us.

When he said, then, that we must lose our lives, he must have been referring to that part of us that denies this supreme Presence, that part of us that lives contrary to It, that part of us that is out of harmony with It. He really was telling us that there are certain things we have to let go of before we can find our true center — the real spirit and the perfect man which he always assumed to be there.

Jesus said: "Blessed are the meek: for they shall inherit the earth." At first this looks as though he were telling us that we cannot inherit the Kingdom of God until we have first renounced the kingdom of man. Yet we find that he multiplied the loaves and fishes when the multitude was hungry; he turned water into wine at the wedding feast, and in every way seemed to meet human needs whenever they arose. So even in teaching us that we must surrender something he was not telling us that we should live in poverty or limitation. What he really was saying is that when we put our trust in external things alone we are always certain to become disillusioned, for a person may have a fortune one day and lose it in the next; he may have a position of high power and instantly lose all public acclaim.

However, he was telling us about something more real

than this; something which contains everything necessary to living, even in this world. For he knew that we need food and clothing and shelter. He was not saying that the Divine Will imposes suffering on us, but that when we fail to live in accord with the Divine, we bring suffering on ourselves. So we see that losing our lives, or making the great surrender to the Spirit, does not mean losing anything worthwhile. It means getting rid of those things which deny the Presence and the Power of the Spirit right here on Earth. It is the great negations of life that we have to surrender, the doubts and fears and uncertainties, the coldness and unkindness, the lack of love.

All of these negative things Jesus called "sins." But the very word "sin" has been misinterpreted and misconstrued. The original meaning of sin was to miss the mark, to make a mistake, to err in judgment, or to do something that separates us from the conscious daily realization that we already are one with the supreme Giver of life. God is Love and we cannot get close to the nature of love while we hate. It is the hate we have to surrender and not the love. When Jesus said you have to lose your life to find it he was saying in effect: You have to lose your hate if you wish to find love. You have to let go of everything that is unkind if you wish to discover kindness. You have to surrender fear if you wish to discover faith.

It is not easy to make this surrender because we are so in the habit of thinking of ourselves as being such strong, self-reliant personalities that we can sweep everything before us. It is not easy to be meek. But again, we should examine the meaning of meekness. While we do not find any arrogance in the life of Jesus, we always find a terrific strength of character, a will to accomplish what he set out to do, a determination to fulfill his mission. When he said that the meek inherit the earth, he was not saying that we have to be wishy-washy or willy-nilly, but that in true meekness we should recognize that all power finally rests in the

Spirit.

To be meek is to be humble before the truth. A person is truly meek or humble when he looks upon the grandeur of a mountain or the vastness of the ocean or thinks about the bigness of things. He does not become lost in this bigness or this grandeur, but he does stand in awe before it. When he does this, something deep within him responds, something within him embraces the ocean, something within him melts into the mountain, and he becomes one with them. This is true meekness.

Jesus also said: "Blessed are they which do hunger and thirst after righteousness: for they shall be filled." Everyone longs to be made whole; everyone really does hunger and thirst after peace and joy. Jesus used the expression "hunger and thirst" because everyone knows how it feels to be hungry and how it feels to be thirsty. When we are hungry we go in search of food, when we are thirsty we look for water. There is in everyone a deep hunger for another kind of food and a deep thirst for another kind of drink which Jesus said is not only natural to us but necessary for us. For he said that we do not live by bread alone, but by every word that proceeds from the mouth of God.

The true scientific mind hungers after knowledge. A scientist feels incomplete until he has wrested the secrets of nature from the invisible and brought them forth into realities. But in his search he has to surrender all personal opinion, all arrogant attitudes of mind, and in true meekness follow the scientific pathway which leads to the discovery of a principle in nature that he inherits after he has first surrendered himself to it. No one makes a greater surrender than the scientist, for he is always willing to be led by the truth, no matter what path it seems to take. Truth and science, in many ways, mean the same thing, for all scientific research is a process of seeking out the laws of nature, discovering how they work, and then subjecting the individual will to the way they work. It is in this way alone that science makes progress. This is always the path that it follows.

We all hunger and thirst after love because we feel incomplete without it. But have we really looked into the nature of love? Have we followed the method that science, which is a search after truth, finds necessary? We hunger and thirst after love but how often do we follow another thought of Jesus where he said: "Greater love hath no man than this, that a man lay down his life for his friends"?

We cannot suppose that Jesus meant that we really give up our lives because this would serve no good purpose. It would not help the world for all the good people to suddenly die. It would impoverish it more than any other one thing that could happen. Jesus must have meant, then, that we lay down everything that constitutes the great unreality, the great lie, the great separation. Love is kind and we have to lay down all unkindness before we discover love.

We want peace of mind and an inward sense of security. But are we willing to surrender all confusion and discord? We are so full of resistance and combativeness and antagonism. The reason we are over-aggressive is really because we feel so insecure inside. In a sense we put up a big bluff and make a big noise and throw ourselves around just because we are so hurt inside. When we resist a thing we make very real in our imagination that which we are sincerely trying to get rid of and we become a house divided against itself, which Jesus said cannot stand. True non-resistance is the surrender of every arrogant attitude of mind to good, and good alone. Those who have made this surrender have found real peace of mind, happiness, and wholeness in the only place where it can be found, which is within themselves.

We have thought that we must work so hard to attain the Kingdom, there is so much we have to do about it. This has become such a burden on our minds that we have gotten our little human selves so completely in the way that the Kingdom which was given cannot be accepted. Life is the gift of God and not of man. This is why Jesus said that no man has the power to give it or to take it away. Are we, then, willing to let go of this inflated ego of ours, this gigantic make-believe, this mask we wear, this camouflage we put on, and in simplicity accept life?

Therefore, say to yourself, quietly and with deep conviction:

Believing that the Spirit of God is at the center of my being, and believing that the Christ-Spirit dwells within me, I now let the Presence and the Power of the Spirit go before me and prepare my way. Today I am surrendering all doubt and fear to this indwelling Presence. I am loosing everything unlovely from my mind and permitting love to fulfill its Divine purpose through me.

Realizing that this same Spirit must be in all people, I am permitting the Spirit within me to greet the Spirit within others in glad recognition. Knowing that God must be in all people, I am permitting the God within me to reach out to everyone with a feeling of unity, of peace, and of understanding. Realizing that there can be but one Spirit in all things, I am learning to feel the Presence of this Spirit in everything I do.

Knowing that all Power is of the Spirit, I am permitting It to govern and guide, to lead and direct my thoughts and my acts. Feeling that Love is the all-sustaining essence of life, the great Reality, I permit Love to flow through me and embrace the whole world.

To the Spirit that fills everything with Its Presence, and to that Goodness which encircles all in Its loving embrace, I commit myself now and forevermore. And so it is.

CHAPTER III

THE MYSTERY OF MIND

Today it is part of the procedure of a physician to inquire into the emotional reactions of his patient. If we were to say, "I am suffering with insomnia and break out with perspiration in the night and can't seem to get any rest," the doctor might ask how we were thinking in order to find the nature of our inner conflicts. For the doctor knows better than the patient that a sleeping tablet is no final answer to insomnia. So he tries to find out the reason for the restlessness, which is often some form of inner conflict as though the mind were trying to go in two directions at once.

Today, instead of speaking of a healthy mind in a healthy body, we say that there must be a healthy mind before there can be a healthy body.

Surely the mind is an unbelievable thing. Investigations that have been carried on in some universities show that the mind reaches out into the future and can, under certain circumstances, foretell what is going to happen, just as it can reach back into the past and remember what already has happened. The very latest discoveries are collecting much material which leads us to suppose that the mind is not confined to the body at all, but in many respects is independent of it.

No doubt these discoveries will lead us to a complete confirmation of immortality. This investigation is being conducted in a scientific manner independently of any dogmatic beliefs. And the evidence that is piling up will some day completely change our whole outlook on life. We shall come to understand that we are immortal right now. It will show us that all people are immortal, not just some, and this is exactly as it must be for God has no favorites.

I believe it will be shown with equal certainty that our success or failure in life, whether we are happy or unhappy, prosperous or impoverished, is largely due to our mental attitudes, our faith, and our fears.

There is another thing that seems equally true to me: Every man has a direct inlet, somewhere, to the Mind of God. If so, then why should we not become an outlet to the Mind of God? Why should not the Mind of God flow through us and through our actions? Why should not Divine Power animate everything we do? Why should not the Spirit, which is present everywhere, protect and guide and counsel and direct us?

If it has been proved that the mind can look both forward and backward, it has with equal certainty been demonstrated that eternity is God's minute of time and God's minute of time is the time we are living right now. It stretches backward and forward, but it is also present with us. We live in an eternal hour from which we may gather as much experience, as much good or as much evil, as we put into it.

But what is this elusive thing we call our mind? I believe the answer to this question is very simple. It seems to me that God, the living Spirit, can be thought of as a universal Mind flowing through everything and a Divine Power animating everything and an infinite Energy energizing everything. The Mind of God, as a Divine Presence, is so close to us that It really is our mind. I believe there is one Mind, that Mind is God, that Mind is our mind now.

More than anything else Jesus emphasized the thought that God is all there is. More than anyone else Jesus proved his claim. He reached out and touched God in people and in things. And as he did this, the miracle of life took place, the sick were healed, the multitude was fed, and signs and wonders followed.

Everyone thought he possessed a power which others do not have. But he told us that he did not have a power which was withheld from others; that he was using a power which we all have. I have no doubt but that our own well-being and the salvation of the world depends on an ever-increasing number of people trying to find out what Jesus was talking about, coming to believe in his claims, and learning to practice the few simple thoughts he gave us.

Nothing can hinder us but ourselves. We can have faith, if we decide to have it. We can be lovable and kind, if we wish to. We can turn away from fear and doubt, if we will to. But this will-to-believe no one can give to us for how can someone else give us what we already have? The gift of Life was made before ever we were born into this world, it came with us. It has been waiting through all our years of doubt, waiting on our acceptance.

Let us take this out of the realm of mere theory or some beautiful sentiment that sounds good but produces no results. We want to know, with certainty, that there is a place within us where we may dwell under the shadow of the Almighty. Let us daily take time to practice believing that we are an outlet for the Mind of God; believing that there is a love that, coming direct from the heart of the Universe Itself, can flow out from us in every direction, blessing everything it touches; believing that there is a certainty that can overcome every confusion and a faith that can destroy all fear. And we must understand that there is a Power operating through, in, and upon our words, our prayers, and our affirmative meditations, and in so doing acts as a Law of Mind. It is something we can depend on with complete certainty.

If, then, we are confronted with confusion, let us get quiet within ourselves and say, "God is not confused, so why should I be? I believe there is an infinite Peace flowing through me, and I am letting this Peace flow out into everything I do. Moreover, I am stating definitely to every confusion in my mind, or to all confusion around me, 'Be still and know that I am God'." When we say, "Be still and know," let us know that something is going to happen, something definite and positive and sure, because it will if we let it.

When we do not know just what to do, let us say, "But the Mind of God in me does know what to do. It not only knows what to do, It is flowing through me now telling me what I ought to do. It is not only telling me what I ought to do, It is impelling me to do it."

When we say, "Something within me knows what to do and impels me to do it," we should turn to any thought that denies this and say, "Now you get out of here. You do not belong here at all. Just run away and mind your own business, I will have nothing to do with you." If we do this we will discover that our affirmative thoughts erase the negative ones. They are just not there any more.

Just do it! And gradually a certainty, an assurance will come to us. With it we will see signs following our belief. They will be definite and positive. We will see conditions change with the change of our belief. The time will come when we will no longer flounder around in doubt or despair, for we will have learned the great secret of secrets, the secret of Life Itself: Each one of us is one with God, now.

Through prayer and in meditation we unify ourselves with the Divine Presence in everything. We come into closer contact with the living Spirit which is in all people and in all things. There is but one final Presence and one final Power in all the Universe. Let us see if we cannot more completely enter into union with Life. Let us see if we cannot more completely feel that Life is flowing out through us into our acts.

Therefore, say to yourself, quietly and with deep conviction:

I know that the Divine Spirit is operating through me now. I know that I am not limited by anything that has happened, or by anything that is now happening. I am aware that the Truth is making me free from any belief in want, lack, or limitation. I have a feeling of security and of ability to do any good thing that I should do.

I am entering into an entirely new set of conditions and circumstances. That which has no limit is flowing through my consciousness into action. I am guided by the same Intelligence and inspired by the same Imagination which scatters the moonbeams across the waves, and holds the forces of nature in Its grasp. I have a calm, inward conviction of my union with good, my oneness with God.

I have complete confidence that the God who is always with me is able and willing to direct everything I do, to control my affairs, to lead me into the pathway of peace and happiness. I free myself from every sense of condemnation, either against myself or others. I loose every sense of animosity.

I now understand that there is a Presence and a Principle in every person gradually drawing him into the Kingdom of Good. I know that the Kingdom of God is at hand, and I am resolved to discover this Kingdom, to possess It, and to let It possess me, now. And so it is.

CHAPTER IV

AN ADVENTURE IN FAITH

Jesus told us not to judge according to appearances because there is a perfection at the center of things. This is what he meant when he said: "Be ye therefore perfect, even as your Father which is in heaven is perfect." He was speaking to the outer man when he said, "Be ye perfect." He was really telling human beings that they ought to be perfect because the Father within them already is perfect.

It seems to me that the only way we can translate the meaning of these words is to accept them in their simplicity and interpret them as though they actually meant what he said. For Jesus never wasted time in idle talk. The more we study the simplicity of his style, the more we discover that it reached to the very foundation of Life Itself, and that among all the great teachers of the ages Jesus had reduced his spiritual philosophy to a few simple, fundamental facts which he taught and which he lived. He actually believed that there is a spiritual center within everyone and that when the intellect, the will, and the feeling make a complete surrender of littleness, fear, and doubt, it will discover something at the center of its own being that is big and adequate and already whole.

This inner center of our being is what is meant by the word Christ, the Anointed or the Illumined. And this is why one of the followers of Jesus said that we should put off the old man, which of course means all our fears and follies, and put on the new man, which is Christ. Christ means God-in-us. It means the Divine Son at the center of every person's life.

If Jesus was right, we are both safe and sane when we believe there is a perfection forever established, a Kingdom of God forever at hand, and a possibility of good which is available right now. But Jesus was more than a great spiritual thinker. He was practical. He was confronted by people then, as he would be now, who were sick, impoverished, and unhappy, by those who had lost hope and the enthusiasm and joy of living. It was to these common people that he spoke. It was to them that he ministered. He taught in the fields, out on the desert, as he walked by the wayside, on the crowded street corner, and by the shores of the lake.

Since the teachings of Jesus contain the key to right living, it is well to consider their meaning. In doing this we should forget all our long arguments and controversies because they are of no importance at all. We should re-read the words of Jesus as though we had never heard of them before — start all over again, get a completely fresh outlook. I am sure, if we do this, we will soon find that his teaching was simplicity itself.

Jesus said in effect: God has made you. The Divine Spirit is already within you. This is your Father in your heaven who desires only your good. The Spirit has already provided a Law of Mind, giving you the use of a Power greater than you are. And if you will only learn to live in recognition of this Presence and in harmony with this Law, then the miracle of life and love will take place and you will find that you are free. This is what he meant when he said: "And ye shall know the truth, and the truth shall make you free." He coupled the knowledge of spiritual truth with the thought that there is a Law of Mind which acts upon our belief and brings into our experience those things which we believe.

It might be a little strange to say that Jesus was the greatest psychologist who ever lived, but he was. It might seem more strange to say that he told us all about psycho-somatic medicine, but he did. And it might seem even more difficult to believe that Jesus actually told us that there is a key to successful living because there is a Law of Mind which we can use.

We should realize that Jesus was not talking about any particular age. He was not talking about just himself. For over and over again he said that what he did we could do also, that what he was we may become. It is exactly as though he were to come among us today and say: "You are poor and sick and weak and unhappy. You don't know how to get along with each other. Problems of human existence are so great that you sit down in despair in the midst of your trouble."

But it is also as though he were proclaiming: "This is all unnecessary. There is a Presence within you that is already perfect. You need not worry over your previous mistakes, nor live in anxious anticipation of tomorrow. All you have to do is to learn to live right today. And when you do, previous mistakes will be blotted out and your future will be taken care of."

But before this can happen we must learn to live right today. It is in this moment of time that we are to make the great decision. It is in this day in which we now are liv-ing that we must choose what path we are to follow. Shall we live in fear or in faith? Shall we live in confusion or in the peace which comes from a deep and abiding conviction that there is a Power greater than we are, ready, willing, and able to work for us? I think the outstanding thing in the new spiritual outlook of today is that we are called on to invite this Presence, to experiment with this Power, and actually to live as though God were present with us right now.

But we should not expect to change our whole mode of thinking in a moment's time. Even Jesus grew in grace with God and man. And frequently he told his followers that it might take time and effort to bring about the greatly desired change. He said: "Howbeit this kind goeth not out but by prayer and fasting." What he meant was that sometimes when we are confronted with great difficulties, seem to be surrounded by much confusion, don't feel well physically, and when we are discouraged and distraught, these conditions are overcome by prayer.

After carefully going over all these teachings of Jesus and listening to his wisdom again, we cannot help but realize that he is really telling us how to change our mode of thinking, how to set up a new polarity in the mind which will attract the good we desire rather than repel it. Jesus seemed to have laid no restriction on the willingness of this Power greater than we are to operate for us other than that everything we think and say and do should be based in a consciousness of love, in a realization that we must become one with others even as we already are one with God. This is why he prayed "that they may be one, even as we are one."

The training of the mind to think differently is simple enough, but I would not say that it is easy, for a thing can be simple without being easy. And again this is where faith must be used, faith in a Power greater than we are, based on the firm conviction that we live in a Divine Presence which wishes only good for us, and that God has intended that every man should be well and happy and successful.

Common sense should teach us that we did not create the Universe, nor need we be responsible for the laws of nature. All we can do is to use them. But perhaps we have

30

been using them wrongly in our ignorance, and now we are called on to reeducate our minds, to reform all our thinking, to make a complete and final surrender of all our littleness and fears and doubts and uncertainties to that great Something within us that is calm and certain and sure, that Something that has never really left Its Divine Kingdom even though our minds have become so confused, so unhappy, and so filled with fear.

This is the great challenge. It is also the great adventure — the adventure of faith in a Power greater than we are, the challenge of a Love that abides forever.

Therefore, say to yourself, quietly and with deep conviction:

I realize that I am one with the eternal newness of Life. All that Spirit is creates in and through me. My body is alive with the Life of God. My body is illumined by the Light of God. There is no darkness of discouragement, despair, or defeat. My mind is refreshed in that one Mind that eternally gives of Itself to Its creation.

All that the Father has is mine. I open my heart to accept the good gifts of joy, happiness, and enthusiasm, right now. I open my heart to know that That which is forever ageless is my source.

I decree that my body and my experiences shall reflect the image of Life in all of Its newness, and I shall move through the days of my years with gladness in my mind. I shall dwell in the house of the Lord forever, knowing that my cup is full to overflowing with the only Life there is — the life and the eternal youth of God. And so it is.

CHAPTER V

THE MIND AT WORK

We all should be interested in learning how to use our minds in the most effective way; to know how to think in such a manner that our lives will be happy and successful. And learning how to think rightly is like learning how to use any other set of tools.

Most of us have felt that our lives are governed by our conscious thoughts, but it is now believed that almost ninety percent of our lives are controlled by habit patterns of thought.

Habit thought patterns are different from our conscious thinking. For example, when we drive an automobile we do not consciously think about applying the brake if we see a red traffic signal. The action of our foot on the brake is automatic. This action has been repeated so often that the driver no longer has to think about it. A habit has been formed and the habit pattern takes control of his actions as though some force or power other than himself were operating.

This matter of habits relates to almost every phase of our lives. If we are going to get the most out of our mental tools we should understand how thought patterns are established and what kind of thought patterns are best for us to live by.

One of the outstanding psychologists of our day experimented with a patient by shining a light in front of his eyes. At the same time that the light was turned on to make the pupils of his eyes contract, a bell was rung. This was repeated many times. And each time this happened the pupils of his eyes contracted.

After this had been repeated a sufficient number of times to have trained the person to react in a certain way, another step was taken. The patient was given a switch, which controlled both the light and the bell. When the doctor would say the word "contract" the patient would close his hand, squeezing the switch which turned on the light and rang the bell. When this was done the pupils of his eyes again contracted.

After this was done often enough to have established a habit, the light and the bell were both taken away, as was also the switch. Then an interesting thing was noticed in the experiment. The doctor would just say to the patient, "Contract!" and the patient would close his hand, as instructed, and the pupils of his eyes would contract. To make the experiment even more complete, the patient was then told not to close his hand while the doctor simple said the word "contract" and at this command the pupils of his eyes would contract.

Up to this point there is one thing that we should notice about these experiments. They have all been built and carried out on a basis of suggestion. But here, it seems to me, is the place where the most revealing part of the power of mind enters into the experiment. Finally the doctor simply sat down by his patient and *thought* the word "contract." And the pupils of the patient's eyes contracted.

Does this not indicate the oneness of mind? Not too long ago it would have seemed beyond the realm of imagination that one person could think a certain thing and have another person respond to it. This could not happen unless there were but One Mind, a Unity of which each of us is a part.

We have been accustomed to think that you have a mind, and I have a mind, and our friend has a mind, but the evidence now shows us that there is but One Mind and each of us, in his own different way, uses It. And our use of It is mostly in the formation of habits. The doctor's patient had established the habit of responding, physically, to a certain word. The word was "contract" and the response was the contraction of the pupils of the eyes.

Would it not be interesting to find out how many of us have certain command words or situations or conditions to which we respond in certain ways. We would probably learn that almost every moment of the day we are unconsciously listening to some kind of command and responding to it in exactly the way we have been trained to respond.

Think how we react to such words as "weariness," "fatigue," or "sorrow." And then contrast how differently we respond when we hear words like "wonderful," "beautiful," "happiness," "peace." In each case these are commands that we have learned to react to in a certain way. It is little wonder that Jesus said: ". . . the words I speak unto you, they are spirit, and they are life."

The reason that anyone reacts to a subconscious command or a habit is because he has accepted the command without reservation. He has taken it into the very depths of his mind. Now that he has done this the thought pattern takes control and works for him; he doesn't even have to think about it. The wonderful part of this is that we can use this technique of building habits to bring good things into our lives, to enjoy happiness, health, and success. If we want to form these new thought patterns we simply begin to use new command words and persist until they work automatically for us. So let us go about this in a direct way. Let us stop for a moment and examine our words, our own commands.

How many of us are listening to the confusion of the world and the words that go to make up this confusion? Even in the face of all of this confusion we can still speak a word of peace, and we can speak a word of peace with authority because we know that behind humanity's conflicts there is always the peace of God which is never disturbed by our strife. When we become disturbed inside about anything, then is the moment to be still and say "Peace!" And when we are afraid of anything, then is the time to speak the word "Faith!" When we become angry or listen to the words of hatred, then is the moment to use the word "Love!"

It is not enough simply to do this once or twice, but each of us must discipline himself so that he persists in using these creative spiritual commands. We must do it over and over again until what was at first a conscious and deliberate effort to speak the good word becomes so embodied in our minds, so completely accepted, that there is nothing within us that argues with the good we affirm. We must let the words of "Peace" and "Faith" and "Love" become so deeply seated in our minds that we use them automatically. When we have acquired this spiritual habit we shall discover that our experience responds to the words we use in exactly the same way we use them.

Our freedom to choose words of power and life is the gift of God, a gift so freely given but so seldom used. Now we wish to use this power so that we may get more out of life and contribute more to it.

Therefore, say to yourself, quietly and with deep conviction:

There is a spiritual 'command to which I listen and to which I shall respond. From this moment I shall speak the words of love and life and peace clearly and with authority for all my experience. No matter what happens around me, no matter what happens in the world, I know that this thing called Life is forever proclaiming Its own wholeness through me.

I listen to the still small voice as it speaks within and I proclaim its words of "Love" and "Life" and "Peace" so that they become life and power to me. As they become life and power to me, they bless those around me. They bring happiness and confidence and joy and health to those for whom I speak my healing words. Just as the Father has given me of His life, so may I give faith and hope and love to the world in which I live. And so it is.

CHAPTER VI

GOD AND DR. EINSTEIN

After many years of patient work Dr. Albert Einstein said that there must be one law governing all physical phenomena. If so, it will be one of the greatest and most important discoveries of all time.

Is it any different to say that there must be one law governing all physical phenomena or to say with Emerson, "There is one mind common to all individual men"? The universe is a spiritual system. It is a manifestation if Divine Intelligence. Another world-famed scientist has said that we can think of the universe in the terms of intelligence acting as law, which means mind in action. And still another has said that we can think of the universe in the terms of an infinite Thinker thinking mathematically, which means that faith acts as a law. This is why prayer can be answered.

I would like for us to consider another of Dr. Einstein's propositions: that energy, which is invisible, and mass, which is visible, are interchangeable. Is this any different from the Bible saying: "In the beginning was the Word . . . and the Word was made flesh . . . ."? The thought of God becomes form. What we see comes out of what we do not see. The invisible becomes visible through the Law of Mind. This is what is back of psychosomatic medicine. Thoughts are things in that mental states produce definite results. This is why we meditate, pray, and affirm the presence of good in our lives.

The cause of everything is hidden. What we experience outwardly is a result of silent but intelligent forces that operate on the invisible side of life. So far as you and I are concerned, our minds represent this invisible side of life. Another great scientist, Dr. Gustaf Stromberg, said in his book, *The Soul of the Universe*, that there is an invisible pattern for everything in the visible world. This is no different from the Bible statement that the invisible things of God are made manifest by the visible. Everything, including our own being, is rooted in, and draws life from an invisible Source. Paul said: "There are also celestial bodies, and bodies terrestrial . . . there is a natural body, and there is a spiritual body."

We need not feel that our faith is without reason, or that the hope within us is unjustified. Of course we know that everything does not appear right in the world in which we live. There is much that ought to be changed. But if we can find a faith and a conviction based on law, as well as intuition and inspiration, then we can reinterpret the wonderful thoughts of Jesus in a new light and come to realize that destiny is not a thing in itself but is merely the way we are using the Law of Life, the Power greater than we are. We are not pawns on a checkerboard of fate. We are persons in our own right. If we have been using the Law of Life in such a way as to produce harm, we can reverse the process and as easily bring about harmony in our lives.

But the skeptic may say that this is too good to be true. May I ask this: Is modern invention too good to be true? Are the things being worked out in modern laboratories real or unreal? There is only one answer to this: They are real enough and we are merely discovering the possibilities of life. There are great spiritual and mental laws that govern everything and we really are living in the Mind of God, right now. There is a Power for good available to all of us. Life has willed it this way and we cannot change it. There are two things we can do. We can live in harmony with the Law of our being, or, by opposing It, live in unhappiness until through suffering we learn how better to use that Power of God that flows through us.

The one sure thing that every man possesses, and that no man can rob him of, is the self; that Something within, the Spirit of God at the center of every man. We should learn to trust the self because we first have faith in God. Take time each day to reaffirm our intimate relationship to the Spirit; act as though we were the son of God, and we will surely discover that we are. Inspiration, hope, and joy will come with this revelation.

This is the secret of life, the pearl of great price that we are to treasure in our innermost being, even as we share it with others. For the love we have for them will come back to us multiplied and the good we set in motion will return to us a thousandfold. This is the way of life. This is the law of our being. This is what the saints, the sages, the poets, the wise, and the good of the ages have known. This is what Jesus taught. This is what is true. This is what we must believe.

Therefore, say to yourself, quietly and with deep conviction:

"In the beginning was the Word, and the Word was with God, and the Word was God." I now completely accept that the Law of God is operating through me; that I am using a Power greater than I am. I have complete belief in this Power.

I believe that the Law of Mind will bring into my experience, and into the experience of those I am thinking of, everything that makes life worthwhile. Wishing only the good and seeing only the good, I believe that this good which I wish for others and see for myself will return to me. It blesses everyone it contacts, everyone I am thinking of. It also blesses me, personally and directly.

I pass all of my affairs over into the keeping of Divine Intelligence. Letting go of all doubt or uncertainty, I enter into faith and conviction, into the expectancy of good, into the acceptance that the Kingdom of God is really at hand. I affirm that I live, move, and have my being in this Kingdom, here and now.

It is my choice that the Presence and the Power of this Kingdom shall dominate my life, causing it to be happy and to give happiness to others, causing me to love and to be loved, helping me to proclaim the good news that the Kingdom of God is at hand. And so it is.

CHAPTER VII

THE GREATEST THING IN LIFE

Everyone loves a lover. No matter what our faults may be, if we have a deep affection for people they will excuse our shortcomings. Those who have had the greatest love for humanity are the ones we admire the most. Love is the greatest thing in life and without it we are lost.

The appeal that Lincoln had was his love for others, his sincere desire to be helpful and understanding, and the spirit of tolerance which he maintained even with his enemies. Of course, the outstanding example in all history is Jesus, who told us that we should even love our enemies and do good to those who dislike us.

Those who refuse to love others never get much out of life, while those who feel the lack of being loved are in an equally bad position for they generally have an unconscious sense of being rejected, not wanted, and not needed. People who have neurotic tendencies generally are those whose thinking is so centered on themselves that it is hard for them to include others in their lives.

To learn to love rightly and well, then, is one of the greatest lessons in life. If we admire people and if we do have deep affection for them, why should we hesitate to express it?

Why should we refuse to use the greatest thing we possess, the ability to put ourselves in the other person's place and meet him as we would like him to meet us?

Jesus knew what we all must learn: that we cannot really have an attitude of dislike or hate or viciousness toward other people without robbing ourselves of the healing power and the comforting Presence and the Divine Assurance that the universe itself rests on the shoulders of Love. Jesus was more than a sentimentalist. He plainly said that we must reap as we sow, and that if we would receive the gifts of life we must be equally willing to distribute them. He knew that that which is withheld from others is also withheld from ourselves.

Love is the greatest of all healing agencies. A vast majority of our physical disorders can, to some degree, be traced back to an inward sense of insecurity. Love creates confidence; confidence gives self-assurance based on a Power greater than we are, and self-assurance is necessary to any successful life.

But love is also forgivingness. Love overlooks the little differences that we have and finds a point of reconciliation with others. Love creates tolerance and human understanding, without which we become really divided against ourselves and without which we almost unconsciously become filled with criticism, condemnation, and false judgment. No one can be happy or enjoy the greatest fulfillment in life until he has come to see that most people try to do about the best they can. And when we are able to reach out beyond the indifference and the coldness of life, reach through all intolerance and unkindness, only then do we meet that Divine center which is forever established within every person.

We know from experience that when we become upset, as we all do, over problems which we do not know how to meet, the best thing we can do is to find someone to whom we can talk who has a deep understanding of life, a great tolerance for living, and who in his own experience has learned that just simple human kindness is the greatest thing on earth. This is why people who believe that God is love, who persist in maintaining an attitude of goodwill toward others, meet others on a common basis of sympathy, kindliness, and understanding.

An idea I would like to introduce is that since the very nature of our being is rooted in the need to love and be loved, we are perfectly right in assuming that God is Love. How could we possibly think of a God who could be either unkind or unloving?

We should no longer feel that there is a God who seeks retribution or that there is any Divine Power that would consign or condemn anyone to a state of perpetual unhappiness. While it is true that as a man sows so must he also reap, it is also true that when he stops sowing discord he will begin to reap harmony, when he stops sowing hate he will begin to reap love, when he stops sowing fear he will begin to reap faith.

Jesus introduced the idea of a Divine forgivingness based on his belief in a Divine Love and told us that when we find the one we shall also discover the other. This is why he forgave the man who died on the cross next to him and said to him: "To day shalt thou be with me in paradise." He never even intimated that anyone would be punished for his mistakes when he stopped making them, nor did he ever suggest that this world and the life we live here was the only place where we could stop making mistakes. Jesus viewed this life merely as an introduction to another one, a prelude to a larger life. He said: "In my Father's house are many mansions: if it were not so, I would have told you."

We must realize, then, that Divine Love and Divine Forgivingness reach even beyond the grave and that there is no place where they will ever stop. We have all made so many mistakes in this life, because of human ignorance, and we have all done so many things that we ought not to have done, that unless we can feel that love and forgivingness are eternal we should store up such a sense of condemnation within ourselves that we could not come to the point where we could even forgive ourselves for our own mistakes. And if we could not forgive ourselves, we should always have an unconscious feeling that God, or the Divine Giver, does not forgive us.

Jesus taught three great truths, and we find them running through everything he said. The first, of course, is that God is all there is, whether it is here or hereafter. God is Life. God is Good. The Divine forever gives of Itself to us.

The next is that there is a Power greater than we are and a Law of Mind which we are all using, whether or not we are aware of the fact. He told us exactly what this Law is and how to use It. And he said It will never fail us because it is done unto us as we believe.

Perhaps the third is even more important than the other two: Jesus taught that the Divine Giver is also the great Forgiver, and that love will finally heal every wound, somewhere, sometime, somehow, either here or hereafter.

There had been other great spiritual teachers before Jesus who were good and wise, but never before or since has the world been given such a complete philosophy of life or such a perfect idea of the relationship that we have with God, the Giver; the Law of Mind that operates for us, and the Divine Love and Forgivingness that must finally win in the life of everyone and bring all people at last into the Kingdom of Good. Since God is the great Giver, we shall have to give if we hope to receive, and since God is the great Forgiver, we shall have to forgive if we wish to be forgiven.

We may delay the day of our freedom, our greater happiness, but somewhere along the line it is destined that we shall discover the Kingdom of God in joy, and live with each other in peace and happiness. It is destined that every man shall finally gain complete freedom from all limitation.

I believe that the time will come when our whole thought

of God will so change that there will never again be anything harsh or unkind in it. We shall learn the lesson of love, the love that we have the need of and the love that we must give if we wish to experience love. I think we shall learn that when we find good in everything we shall receive good from everything. Not in a distant by-and-by, but in an eternal here and an everlasting now.

Knowing that the Law of God is a law of love and of liberty we are seeing freedom and joy and happiness and peace and wholeness in everything we look at. We are responding to the Divine calm which is at the center of everything. And knowing that perfect love casts out all fear, we are strong and confident because we know that the Law of God goes with us and prepares the way before us.

Realizing that the kingdom of love is at hand today, we enter into this kingdom with a song of praise, a hymn of joy. Knowing that God is hid in everything, we reveal this Divine Presence to ourselves and to each other, in sympathy, in love, in kindness.

Knowing that the great Giver is also the Divine Forgiver, we release everything that denies this Divine givingness. We forgive ourselves and everyone else for any mistakes we may have made. We unburden our minds and free our hearts, and we enter into the consciousness of Good which includes all people, all events, all things, everything, everywhere.

So we give back to the Divine Presence that which It has given to us, knowing that the gift will again be returned, and multiplied. So shall peace and joy come as a light from heaven. In that light let us walk.

Therefore, say to yourself, quietly and with deep conviction:
Believing that God is all the Presence there is, I feel this Presence in everything and in everyone.

Dwelling on the thought that God is Love, I permit my mind to become filled with the consciousness of this Love. I permit this Love to envelop everything and everyone, bringing with it a sense of peace and joy and certainty.

Realizing that God is Life, I open my thought to such a complete inflowing of this Divine Life that I see It and feel It everywhere, the one perfect Life which is God, in people, in nature, animating every act, sustaining all movement. My faith in this Life is complete, positive, and certain.

Knowing that all things are possible to faith, I say to my own mind: Be not afraid. Faith makes my way certain. Faith goes before me and prepares the way.

Beliving that God is in everyone, I meet Him in people and I am one with everyone I meet. Knowing that God is Peace, I open my mind to the quiet influence and the calm certainty of Peace. Knowing that God is Joy, I meet every situation in happiness. I recognize that Life within me can do all things with complete assurance, and does guide me with assurance into a greater experience of love and good. And so it is.

CHAPTER VIII

HIDDEN THOUGHTS

Who would stand in front of an automobile and let it run over him just for the fun of it? Or jump off a roof and break a leg merely to take a rest cure in a hospital?

It is said that eighty percent of all accidents are unconsciously invited. "Unconsciously invited" is not such an innocent term as it seems to be, because it deals with the fact that nine-tenths of our thinking is not even conscious. We do not consciously think of driving our cars, or walking down the street, or having our food digest, or making our hearts beat.

Just as there are automatic reactions in our physical body, so there are deeper automatic reactions in our mind. Our mind is really the creative thing within us. But what has this to do with accidents? Well, let us see! It is now known that when we unconsciously look forward to more trouble than pleasure from some particular incident, we unconsciously try to avoid that situation.

For instance, a person starts down the street on an important mission but perhaps he feels it is a situation that he fears he cannot quite handle. He is not willing to admit this because then he would be calling himself a coward and we all need self-esteem. But his subconscious reaction, without the consent of his intellect or conscious awareness, causes him to fall down and break his arm, his leg, or his nose.

His emotional, unconscious desire has won over his intellect. It has seen to it that he need not meet a situation which he is unconsciously afraid of. One of the axioms of Coué was that when the will and imagination are in conflict, the imagination and not the will always wins. Such is our nature. It is well known that this can be carried so far that perhaps instead of meeting with an accident he might be seized with a physical ailment.

This mind of ours is a pretty terrific thing. If it can produce eighty percent of our accidents, what else can it do to us? There is no question but that it governs the unconscious functioning of the body, all these silent forces that conspire to maintain our physical well-being.

The Bible says: "As [man] thinketh in his heart, so is he." And Jesus, the most enlightened of all men, said that it is done unto us as we believe. But Jesus did not explain to his followers that ninety percent of their belief was unconscious. It has taken the world two thousand years to discover this. But does this mean that we are to be afraid of the unconscious workings of our mind? Of course not. Because the very fact that the mind is creative shows that we are persons in our own right. If we were not creative we merely would be mental automatons, robots, nonentities. We would not be persons at all; we would be like cogs in a wheel or bolts in a piece of machinery, and this is not what Life has intended for us at all.

When Life created us It gave us the two great endowments of God, the two highest gifts of heaven: love and creativity. Love, so that we may have confidence in life, a sense of security, and peace and joy in living; creativity, so that we can really live as persons and express ourselves individually. Life has done very well by us. Would it be too much to say that God has given us the best He has and then let us alone to discover ourselves?

We are somebody. I am glad that we are. I would rather have this creative Thing within me, even though It does produce a pain now and then, or break a toe or two, than to be without It. After all, It is the Thing that painted all the madonnas and built all the cathedrals. It is the Thing that made all the inventions and wrote all the books. We should not be afraid of this creative Thing in us for It is the greatest gift of Life.

God never makes any mistakes and there are no accidents in the Divine Life. Everything is so ordained that when we learn to make a right use of the laws of Life, freedom, love, beauty, happiness, and wholeness must follow, because Life Itself is neither weak, unhappy, nor inadequate.

The Law of Mind, like all other laws in nature, is automatic. If we plant a cabbage seed we get cabbage; the law is neutral. Plant a seed of uncertainty in our mind and we might get an accident. If we plant a rosebush in the same soil that the cabbage came from, we will have roses. Plant a seed of faith and confidence and we will experience happiness. It is a funny thing, this mind of ours; and there seems to be nothing we can do about it other than learn how it works and then use it constructively.

Just as there is a mind in us that can do all these things, and do them automatically, just so is there a Mind around us that governs everything in our life. When we come to know God in the right way, and come to have confidence in Life, intelligently, constructively, and with a deep and biding faith, It converts all that is negative in our experience into that which is positive, all that is evil into good, all that seems a failure into success. Give and we will be given to. Love and we will be loved. Enter into peace and we will be come peaceful.

This is the way God has made us; this is what Life has

given us; this is the way we are. Deep within us there is a place of peace, of calm, and of security, where trouble and accidents do not occur, where truth and love reign supreme, and where good only is power.

Therefore, say to yourself, quietly and with deep conviction:

I know that all the Power there is and all the Presence there is, is Love, the living Spirit. I know that Love is Divine protection and that I am governed, guided, and guarded into the pathways of peace, of joy, and of security.

I know that there is no confusion or doubt in the Mind of God, and God's Mind is the only Mind there is. This Mind is my mind now, directing everything I do, guarding every movement I make. For "Her ways are ways of pleasantness, and all her paths are peace." I know that this is true of all people. This is what I believe about everyone. This is what exists for the whole world.

This is my prayer of acceptance today and every day. I feel safe in the keeping of Divine Love and infinite Power. I feel the soft enveloping presence of the living Spirit. And so it is.

CHAPTER IX

IDEAS FOR LIVING

Too long we have held the teaching of Jesus in a vague and abstract way, not realizing that he told us how to live, right here and now, in happiness, in wholeness, and in prosperity.

He never would have healed the sick unless he had known that disease is unnatural to the Spirit. He would not have fed the multitude unless he had known that Divine Providence ordained that the food we need to sustain physical life should be provided.

He never would have forgiven people their sins to the last moment of their human existence, as he did with one who died with him on another cross, unless he had known that the eternal Heart forever forgives and unless he knew that all men are immortal and destined to live forever, somewhere.

Jesus, the kindest soul who ever lived, would never have misled people by telling them that there is a Power for good greater than they are that they can use when he said: " . . . as thou hast believed, so be it done onto thee" unless he had known that there is a spiritual Law that can be used for every good purpose.

He had no long-drawn-out dogma, no set of creeds. He

was a person who was acquainted with God, who was able to feel and see God in everything and in everyone. We should return to the simple teaching of this enlightened man who gave the world the greatest truth it has ever had.

Jesus taught that there is justice in the universe without judgment; that we are all blessed by the good we do, and that we are stopped when we seek to do evil. He knew that finally everyone must come to see this. Just as surely as we live, the time will come when the whole thought of punishment in the hereafter will be obliterated from the human mind.

But how are we to balance this with justice? The answer is simple: While we cause others to shed tears, we ourselves shall shed them. This is punishment enough.

We cannot say to a person filled with hate that God forgives him in his hate. We can only say: "God is love. You are missing something; you are standing in the shadow of a great Reality. Forgive, and you will be forgiven."

We cannot say to a man who is dishonest that it makes no difference. We can only say to him: "This is your freedom, but remember, while you misuse others, you will be obliged to suffer. Justice demands that you suffer to the day of atonement, which merely means at-one-ment, and the very moment that you stop misusing the Law of God, you will cease suffering."

We cannot intelligently say to anyone: "Because there is no hell and no devil, which there certainly is not, you can act in an evil manner and not suffer." We can only say: "My friend, your heaven and your hell are in your own mind. Perhaps you are in hell at this moment, but how would you like to trade hell for heaven? How would you like to swap the devil for God? How would you like to exchange hate for love, and greed and avarice for Divine Givingness? How would you like to so forgive others that nothing can ever again be held against you?"

There is no such thing as a lost soul. If there were we

would not know where to look for it. I believe, with complete certainty and with equal sanity, that good finally will come to everyone. Jesus said that the Kingdom of God is at hand and that the good we seek already is here, could we see it. For in such degree as we see the Divine Kingdom around us, we shall enter into It. In such degree as we find God within ourselves, and others, we shall be made whole.

Spiritual Healing. Jesus healed the sick through spiritual Law. And he said that we all have access to this Law. Spiritual mind healing has long since passed the experimental stage. There are millions of people in America today who bear witness to this fact. But in dealing with this thing called Life, and the Power greater than we are, and the Law of Mind that we can use, we do not deny that people are sick or that they often need physical attention. A program of spiritual mind healing in no way seeks either to criticize, obstruct, or deny the benefits of medicine, surgery, diet, or sanitation.

We make a simple but honest claim when we say that there are spiritual techniques of healing that can be added to every known system of therapy. These techniques are simple, easy to understand, and anyone can apply them for himself or others.

Divine Guidance for Successful Living. This thing called Life is not only a healing agency for the body and the emotions. It is also sustenance for our daily need in every department of life. There are techniques that are just as definite for drawing on the Mind of God for guidance in our daily activities as there are techniques for healing the body. We know that the person who prays aright can demonstrate his right place in life.

We should not think of Divine guidance as something supernatural, but as completely natural. If we are not experiencing right action and harmony it is because we have lost contact with this thing called Life, which could and should be directing our activities. We believe that no matter what a man's circumstances in life, there is an infinite Intelligence that can take him by the hand and lead him into the path of right action where he will experience success, happiness, and peace.

The Family Life. Nothing is more important than that we should understand how this thing called Life works in the family circle. If we can show people that each member of the family is rooted in one Divine Presence, and teach them tolerance, love, and mutual understanding, we will have cooperation in the family. The family life has little chance of success without God.

Substance and Supply. Jesus told us that there is a Law of Mind which is always available, which can bring to us everything necessary for our well-being. He used this Law to meet the need when the need arose. When they wanted money, he found it in a fish's mouth; when they needed wine, he turned water into wine; and when the multitude was hungry, he fed them. We rob no one when we are successful, rather, we add to the sum total of all human good.

Love and Friendship. Too many people are lonely and without friends. It is natural that everyone should seek friendship, for the life without love is empty. There is a Law of Mind which can heal loneliness and bring love and friendship into the life of everyone.

Overcoming Fear. Fear is the greatest enemy of man, and yet Jesus said: "Fear not, little flock; for it is your Father's good pleasure to give you the kingdom." Jesus did not even say that we have to earn this Kingdom, for he knew that God is the eternal Giver. He knew that the gift of life already has been made, even though it has not been fully received.

Forgiveness. The great Giver is also the great Forgiver. Jesus said that we must forgive if we would be forgiven; that hate, envy, and resentment must be banished from the mind if we would live in peace and security. We are all on the pathway of evolution and we all make mistakes and we all need to be forgiven for them. Let us learn, then, to forgive others that we ourselves shall be free from the burden of guilt.

Personality. Everyone has a personality, be it good, bad, or indifferent. But back of this personality there is a Divine, God-ordained individual, a real person, a spiritual ego. Too often our objective, and even our mental and emotional personalities tend to mask or cover rather than reveal that unique something which the Mind of God has implanted within each one of us.

To find our true center is one of the great quests of life. To discover God within is the greatest thing that could happen to anyone. The miracle which follows such discovery changes the whole personality, a new power surges into it through the revelation of the Divine Presence at the center of its own being.

We do not need to imitate others or to shape our lives according to their thoughts. All we have to do is to learn to be ourselves, for there is at the center of everyone's life, behind the mask he wears, an eternal Son of the living God. It is this Son that we wish to reveal.

The Law of Giving and Receiving. Jesus said: "Give, and it shall be given unto you . . . ." This is a law of Life. We should give of ourselves in love and in service to others, in a spirit of generosity and good-fellowship. To refuse to give is to refuse to receive, for everything moves in circles. Real giving is the givingness of the self. A kind word, a thoughtful act, perhaps just a smile, can help lighten the burdens of others.

We are all parts of each other because the same God is in each one of us, wearing a different face. God is the Father of all, in all, and through all, and we are the brothers of all. No man can live unto himself alone. We can only live unto God and unto each other. On this pathway alone is there freedom, joy, and completion. As surely as the eternal circuits of God follow their courses, so shall those who give all, receive all.

Our Country. We believe in America and in what it stands for. We believe that democracy is a spiritual idea and that it is the destiny of our great nation to prove to the world that freedom under law and individual initiative under Divine guidance is the right way of life.

In these troubled times, when the very principles of freedom are being questioned and when people seek to destroy freedom in the name of liberty, it is right and fitting that we should reaffirm our allegiance to the two greatest human documents every written: The Declaration of Independence and the Constitution of the United States with its Bill of Rights. We believe that along this road alone lies the pathway to continual liberty.

Let us be on the alert to refute any and all ideas that seek to dethrone this citadel of liberty, for in eternal vigilence alone can there be perpetual freedom. America is the great dream of the ages. Let us keep this dream fresh and fair in our minds and through our united faith create a spirit of unity and solidarity against which the waves of disruption beat in vain because it is built on the rock of eternal Truth.

Therefore, say to yourself, quietly and with deep conviction:

I know that it is done unto me as I believe. I affirm my faith in the all-sustaining Power of the living Spirit.

I affirm and accept the simple fact that I live and move and have my being in a Divine Presence which is perfect, whose nature is love and peace and joy.

I affirm my conviction that the Heart of the Eternal is most wonderfully kind, and as I accept Its Divine givingness, so in turn do I give to others.

I affirm my conviction that the infinite Giver forever forgives and that I, in turn, forgive myself and everyone else for any mistakes that may have been made.

I affirm the beneficent action of the Divine Presence in every phase of my life. And so it is.

CHAPTER X

THE KINGDOM IS YOURS

"The Kingdom of Heaven" is a subject that has been discussed for generations and each one thinking about it and talking about it discusses it only in his own way. But I shall try to discuss it from an objective viewpoint and see what it seems that it must mean.

Jesus plainly located the Kingdom of Heaven as an inner perception of Life. He did not say that the physical world or the objective world is an unreality. Modern science, in theoretically doing away with the material universe, does not deny that which looks as though it were a material universe. Sir Arthur Eddington, both a scientist and a philosopher, in his book on modern science and metaphysics said that while in all probability we are living in what you and I would call a mental or a spiritual Universe, it does not mean that my thought put the planet Mars where it is, because before I thought somebody else saw it there and if I never experienced its being there, it would be there just the same. There is something there, and it is not an illusion.

The world of Spirit cannot be a world of illusion. Countless generations of people have gazed upon a certain object, an objective fact — a tree, a mountain — and they all have seen the same thing. No one of these people put that object there, and yet we can affirm at the same time that we are living in a spiritual Universe and our reaction to it is mental. We did not put the mountain there, but our relationship to whatever that mountain is is a mental and a spiritual relationship. We may not like it, we may love it; that is our reaction to it. So our thought has never projected the universe in which we live; it has projected our relationship to the universe. Our environment, our reactions to life, our loves and hates and fears, our mistakes, our hopes, our joys — these are our mental experiences in the universe which actually existed before we consciously experienced it.

This is a conclusion of modern science. It is very interesting, one of the most interesting things in the age in which we live, to watch how stealthily but how steadily modern science is gradually entering the back door of ancient metaphysics. It is one of the signs of our times. Every thoughtful, philosophically inclined modern man of science knowns it because although our scientific, theoretical deductions have wiped out the material universe, they have still left everything looking just as it always did look but with a different background in our own imagination. Science, just as metaphysics, is today beginning to think of the universe only in terms of intelligence, but just as that does not deny form, so the metaphysical concept does not deny experience.

The modern physicist tells us that while we theoretically dissolve the material universe, it still leaves us a universe to be experienced, as it should. And when the metaphysician says that theoretically we dissolve everything into Mind and Spirit, it is only the unthoughtful metaphysician who says that all substance is an illusion. If we can see yesterday and today and tomorrow in one sequence, then we see from the viewpoint of the eternal Mind, which sees everything in one sequence, and perfect.

God, seeing the whole as a whole, does not see as we see. "For now we see through a glass, darkly, but then face to face: now I know in part: but then shall I know even as also I am known." If we could see as God sees we should see nothing but a perfect universe. The slow processes of evolution are the result of our perception of the universe, the manifestation of the Mind that is Self-existent. The Kingdom of Heaven will come to each of us, then, not because the Kingdom of God evolves, but because we unfold into the recognition of That which did not have to evolve. I do not think that is speculation; I do not think that has anything to do with an opinion; I think that is so. Every logic, every reason, every penetration of science into the invisible, every revelation in religion, every intuition, every illumination that the world has ever received teaches that. It is a startling thing because it means that just as long as we wait we will be waiting.

I am not one who believes that life is an illusion, or who believes in saying everything is all right when it is all wrong. I do not think that is intelligent. But "the kingdom of God," Jesus said, "is within you." The Kingdom of Heaven is in me; it is in you too, just as much of it, no more of it. My interpretation of it is my individualization of it; your interpretation is yours. One is just as good as another. The Kingdom of God is in each of us and "it cometh not with observation." Emerson said, "A wise old proverb says, 'God comes to see us without bell'." And Edward Roland Sill said, "Peace is already here." It is an awakening, then, to things as they are. This is the first essential of a spiritual conception of the universe.

As we look about and see the apparent tragedy of life — and I do not think we can entirely blind our eyes to it for there is a great deal of suffering in this world — do we always stop to consider that if that suffering were an eternal Reality there would be no escape from it ever? If it were in the Mind of God as an essential necessity there would be no escape. I believe that much that we do and experience in the sight of infinite Intelligence blends into the greater landscape. I fail to see how we can arrive at any intelligent conclusion or perspective of life if we persist in looking at it only from the short-range vision. No man can give any intelligent account of what is going on in the world today unless he does it in the light of the history of the whole human race up until now, a picture which is blotted and blurred when you look at it too closely. No great soul has ever expected the age in which he lived to understand him. He has known that he belongs to the ages; he is speaking an eternal truth. So the tragedy and the pathos and the negations of life, if we can get a broader vision, flatten out and are simply part of the molding process of that individuality and personality which belongs to an eternal and everlasting domain, and is not a creature of time.

It is pathetic that some people have sincerely believed that there are souls that are not immortal. It is unfortunate that anyone has to burden himself with the sense of responsibility for anybody's soul. But the Kingdom of Heaven must be the way God looks at things. God is a unitary Wholeness. Each individual, then, can enter into his kingdom, which is already within him, only in such degree as he sees that he is a part of the whole thing — a part of all Life, wed to It, one with It. We see in each other the reflection or the manifestation of the everlasting Life, and each is an individualized embodiment of It.

Remember, the Kingdom of Heaven is already in us; we are in It; it is only as we are in harmony with It that we awake to It. God is perfect, the Universe is foolproof, everything is all right no matter what it looks like. What are the little chagrins, the little cares, the pettinesses of yesterday? The Kingdom of Heaven is bigger and broader and deeper and wider, and such peace as any man possesses in this world comes from a conscious or unconscious acquiescence with the Universe, a noncombativeness toward It. What if some of us do lose our fortunes? What of it? A shroud has no pockets, a corpse bears nothing with it except its empty nothingness. What I gave away I have; what I kept I lost. That is a law of the Universe. What if we were misunderstood? Emerson tells us that all of the great have been misunderstood. What if we have been inconsistent? Only unwise people think they have to be consistent. We are living in a changing world. Most of the things that seem to make us experience hell are inconsequential.

The Kingdom of Heaven is harmony. It is more than charity. Personally I do not like the word "charity" very much. It is a good word but it is a very limited one. In the evolution of the human race the time will come when charity will no longer be necessary. It is a misconception, but it is good; it rises out of the highest stimulus of spiritual reality. I do not care very much for the word "tolerance" as though we tolerated each other. That is better than intolerance, but' people who are tolerant because they have made up their minds to be tolerant are missing a lot. I like the word "understanding." Everything that is understood will be forgiven. There is no question about that. I am not talking about forgiveness between God and man. God does not have to forgive for God is eternal forgiveness. But everything that we really understand between each other will be forgiven. I do not know when such understanding will come to the world so that nations will be able to lay down their arms. It will come, not today or tomorrow perhaps, as we measure time, but nothing can finally combat it. That process is infinite, painstaking, slow, but certain. Everything that is in line with unity is in the process of winning.

Some day we will come to perfectly appreciate the fact that no living soul is more important than any other one, for in the eternal Kingdom of Reality they are all the same, king and slave, what we call rich and poor, what we call intelligent and unintelligent people, what we call worth-while and not worthwhile people. Right today each one of us is attracting to himself the kind of people and things which are the inevitable correspondents to his inner state of thought. We are told that our conversation should be in heaven. I think that is correct because it is out of such conversation that our thoughts and our convictions come. And out of our convictions come our realizations, and out of our realizations must come our experiences according to Law. Therefore, our conversation should be harmonious.

"The kingdom of God cometh not with observation." This has nothing to do with theology. It existed before Christianity was ever thought of; it would have existed if Jesus had never come to this Earth and there had never been a cross, a crucifix, a prayer, a church, or a creed. Because the Kingdom of God is an eternal state of Being. The Kingdom of Heaven has nothing to do with externalities. It is first of all an inner conviction, next a determination, and then an embodiment. The Kingdom of Heaven is Life, and in such degree as we awake to It, we shall live. It is Abundance, and in such degree as we awake to It we shall have abundance. That is the meaning of the thought to "seek ye first the kingdom of God, and his righteousness; and all these things shall be added unto thee." That is perfectly reasonable. A person who really understands the Kingdom of God and has freed himself from the denial of It will never be in want, for he will be supplied some way. The Kingdom of Heaven would have to be peace, It would have to be happiness, It would have to be joy. I do not think that there is any good thing that could be lacking in the Kingdom of God. And I think that all the world is seeking It. That is why I believe in every man's belief. The Truth is a unitary wholeness; It must contain every good thing, every good and beautiful gift that cometh down from the Father of Life, in which there is no shadow cast by doubt.

The great practical psychological and metaphysical

lesson that we should learn is to speak only an affirmative language. It is written that God's whole language is "Yea" and "Amen." It means exactly what it says, that the Eternal can only have one language and that is an affirmative one. And if we carry it far enough in our thought we will come to the conclusion that the human mind can only affirm, though it can do it negatively as well as positively. I have no question in my mind but that if any individual could become entirely affirmative, he would wipe out every mistake he has ever made and at once be perfect in manifestation. That is why in spiritual healing, in spiritual demonstration, we must plunge beneath the material surface, through the external cause, and get back to the Spirit of the thing which is already perfect, opening avenues in the mind for the greater influx of That which is already there.

The Kingdom of Heaven is a thing to be devoutly experienced. It is the pearl of great price for which a man will sell all that he has in order that he may possess It. And yet It is the only thing that he had before he asked for It. It is the only thing that he possesses that he cannot lose. It is the only thing that is eternal, for It is God incarnated in every living soul. Consequently, It is not an outward pomp or external proclamation, but It is a state of interior awareness coming softly and gently to the soul who recognizes Its presence. If It were an external thing, and not immediately accessible in our own consciousness, we should never be able to find It. It is an idea that conveys us to this place. Heaven is lost for the want of an idea, and the idea that is lacking is the recognition that the work of the Eternal is complete; our evolution consists in our awaking to that which was and is and is to be — "Before Abraham was I am."

Therefore, say to yourself, quietly and with deep conviction:

Today I am letting the Mind of God guide me in everything I think, say, and do. I know that I shall be guided aright; I shall know what to do under every circumstance.

Today I am permitting the Life of the Spirit to energize every atom of my being, knowing that the food I eat, the thoughts I think, and the faith I have, shall be converted into living flesh, radiant with health.

Today I am letting the gladness of the Spirit flow through me, making glad everything I do and shedding gladness on everyone I contact. I am permitting the Love of God to flow from me to all people, embracing them in one universal family which is the household of God.

Today I am opening my mind to the influx of new ideas, knowing that He makes all things new. So shall new thoughts, new ideas, new people, new circumstances come into my experience as I draw upon the invisible forces of my own being — the Love and the Life, the Peace and the Joy which is God, the living Spirit Almighty. And so it is.

CHAPTER XI

SPIRITUAL REALIZATION

The Law of Mind will produce good for us provided we first embody the idea and meaning of it in a spiritual mind treatment. By embodiment we do not mean merely wishing; we mean actual conscious and subjective acceptance of the meaning of the idea. Since Spirit is Life, Love, and Peace, and since It also must be Harmony, one cannot expect to embody spiritual ideas through hatred, confusion, or greed. Spiritual ideas must be spiritually discerned.

We are handicapped in arriving at spiritual realization because of the race belief in imperfection; nor does it necessarily follow that what one person considers normal would be normal to another. No one can expect to demonstrate beyond his ability to rise in awareness to a complete comprehension of the meaning of the idea he wishes to experience. Naturally, an absolute standard of normalcy would be complete perfection. Anything less than this would not be normal to the Spirit.

Each one should seek to know deep within himself that perfection is possible, and in working out his problem he should realize that his experience of imperfection is conditioned by the accumulated race belief inherited from previous generations, plus the effect of the thought atmosphere around him. To realize this is to understand where most of the ideas of imperfection come from. Hence, a person is not discouraged while striving for mastery when he knows that the thought which seeks to limit him arises not from the nature of things but from the mind of man.

There is a pattern of Perfection constantly seeking to manifest through us. But we furnish imperfect conditions through which It must manifest. And since the Law of Mind governing It is always neutral and impersonal, It can manifest for us only through the kind of mental acceptance we furnish for It. The Law provides the method, we furnish the conditions.

Naturally, different types of people furnish different channels through which this infallible Law of Mind operates. The Law completely ignores personal peculiarities and idiosyncrasies. It makes no distinction between individuals, but operates always upon the mental concept established. The Law never shuts anyone out, It includes all people. We are very likely to think that because someone differs from us the Spirit excludes him from reaching his desires until he shifts his way of thinking to more nearly meet our opinions. Yet, the very person whose exterior may grate upon us, may easily be a more perfect channel for the operation of the Law than we are ourselves.

We should be tolerant and be able to meet all kinds and conditions of men, looking through their external differences to the inner sameness and loving all because each is an expression of Spirit. If the Spirit is Peace, we should not permit ourselves to become irritated by others, nor should we withdraw from people because their habits of life are different from ours. The Spirit never withdraws from anyone.

We must not forget that conditions of living change, more or less, in each age. That which one generation regarded as wicked and evil, the following generation óften seeks to emulate. A few years ago a man walking down the street with a twenty dollar gold piece in one hand and a bottle of whiskey in the other, would have been arrested for the possession of the whiskey. Today he would still be arrested, but it would be for the possession of the gold. This does not advocate the use of the whiskey, but rather to show that the human standard of values changes. The person of whom we disapproved twenty years ago, today may have become our closest friend. The world of opinion is a rapidly changing thing and we shall arrive at no stable foundation until we realize the unchanging nature of Reality in the spiritual Universe in which we live.

We should continuously recognize Spirit as the Source of our power. Mind is the agency through which this power flows. Mind is power, and power is Mind. There is no necessity for pleading, begging, or agonizing. We merely recognize power, and open our consciousness to the very fullest capacity to receive it and to allow it to flow.

When we recognize that Spirit saturates every atom in the universe, and incidentally flows through our own body, business, home, and all our external affairs, then we are able to realize that this Source of life is sending power through all these experiences, by and through the Law of Mind. It is the Spirit which is at the very center of all life that we must perceive and accept.

Race belief sometimes asserts itself at this point and raises a doubt: "Perhaps Spirit might not give this power." This is a hangover from our older theological beliefs, the belief that God gives to one and withholds from another, for some inscrutable reason. We must rid ourselves of this notion. We must know that the Law of Mind, controlling our use of universal Power, is entirely neutral, acting in the manner in which It is directed, pouring forth unstintedly through man's decree. There is no need of coercion, nor need there be any feeling of hesitancy as to whether It will act when one needs It. It will act, never fear; man's part is merely to direct It through his spiritual mind treatment. Coupled with this should be an attitude of expectancy of Its activity as a normal procedure. At first there may be something of timidity as an individual begins to do definite work. But gradually, as we find the Law of Mind beginning to act in the direction indicated, we come to know where formerly we merely hoped.

The Law of Mind is the surest thing in the universe. Man's hopes may change, the Law never changes. It knows only one thing: to obey the voice of Spirit. This truth will bear repetition, for it is fundamental. So we should take time to ponder deeply this fact, for upon it rests our entire success in making conscious use of the Law of Mind.

We must not be overly occupied with the details of the manner in which the Law is to work; simply see Its Power resistlessly fulfilling the demand made. We should rest and relax in this assurance, leaving to the Law of Mind the exact details as to how It is to operate for It knows exactly how to go about accomplishing our specific desires. Too often we want to stipulate and outline the exact method, the way a thing should be accomplished. This is not wise, for we are tapping infinite Resources of which we have scarcely had a glimpse. In our treatment unguessed forces may be drawn upon and the answer may come through channels undreamed of by us.

We know that that upon which the mind dwells tends to become objectified in our experience; hence, we should never dwell too much on anything that is negative. Jesus healed disease by a contemplation of perfect health and by an inner sense of certainty that health is normal and natural. He dissipated want through the realization of complete supply. He obliterated hate by refusing to permit it entrance into his consciousness and by dwelling upon the idea of infinite Love. Thus he said to "do good to them that hate you." When we dwell too much upon negative conditions we identify ourselves with them and thus tend to bring into our experience the very thing from which we seek to be freed. Somewhere in a proper spiritual mind treatment we must arrive at the conviction that Spirit is all, It is supreme. Hate is conquered by love, even as fear becomes dissolved in faith. Nor should we feel that we are arraying one power against another.

Spirit has only one mode of action, which is Self-contemplation. It knows only Itself, never anything else. It knows nothing outside of Itself. If It did It would be creating two things, and we would have duality in the universe. This belief in duality is responsible for all the devils, satans, inquisitions, and witch-burnings, for it is a belief in both good and evil. Spirit sees only the good, because It sees and knows nothing but Itself.

Spirit is the essence of all things, but It is never other than Itself, no matter what the form. We therefore look beyond the form to the inner Reality, and know It to be good. Thus we can look into the face of some apparently undesirable situation, and see nothing but God there. In this way we rob it of its fearsomeness. In physical healing we never shudder and say, "My, that is bad," or "serious" or "incurable" or "repulsive." Instead we see the Divine Presence and Perfection in the individual; it is there for that Perfection is the basic Reality and is always present.

The question is often asked, "Did God make the Law of Mind?" The answer is self-evident: The Law of Mind has always existed. It is the mode of action of the Divine Nature and this Law can never fail to operate. This is the secret power of faith, a complete realization that the Law of Mind must work. God, Spirit, or the Divine Presence is ever stimulating our thought. The Law of Mind, obeying the will of this Divine Presence in us, has no choice of Its own. We need never ask, then, does God wish us to enjoy health, happiness, abundance, or to live the good life. The very fact that the Divine Nature is one of perfection and of

70

wholeness, presupposes the necessity that this Divine Nature wishes us everything that is good. The Law of Mind, being neutral, never argues against our desire, but always seeks to fulfill it. Therefore, when our thought is in accord with the Divine Harmony and when we have complete faith and conviction in Its power, then there will be no question whatsoever about the operation of the Law.

Law must always move along the line of our thought. It merely becomes necessary that we understand the meaning of that truth Jesus referred to when he told us that there is a Truth which automatically works for us when we understand It. But there should be no mental reservation in our acceptance of this Truth. We must weed out everything from our thought that questions the ability of our word to become manifest. We should have a complete acceptance of the result of our spiritual mind treatment, and this acceptance is not complete until it becomes embodied without reservation. We shall know when we have done this, for then the desired result does take place because there is no longer anything in our thought which denies the good that our word affirms.

In spiritual mind treatment we should make every endeavor to free ourselves of any sense of strain or anxiety. To accept the results of our treatments with thanksgiving is a scientific approach to Reality. We should seek to develop a childlike trust and a complete simplicity in our awareness of both the Spirit and the Law. The Law does not cooperate with us by the use of many words, but rather, cooperates with us because of the meaning which we give to the words we do use. Anatole France, a master of words, was once asked, "How short can a sentence be and still be effective?" His answer was, "One word, if you can do it." So one word spoken with the deep realization of its meaning is better than thousands of words rattled off without any meaning.

But if we do use the phrase, "God is, and is all there is,"

relative to any particular circumstance, and if this idea that God is all there is seems hazy in our thought, we must continue to meditate upon it until we sense its meaning. The idea must be clear before the Law of Mind can establish it as a concrete and tangible result in our experience. Never forget that we are dealing with an immutable Law of Cause and Effect, and that what we do when we give a treatment is to change some tendency in this Law, some sequence of events, by introducing a realization of Life which automatically dissolves the old sequence and as automatically sets a new one in motion. In doing this we are not changing the Law Itself; we are merely using It in a different way.

Our future is being created out of our present concepts, just as our present experiences are largely a result of what has gone before. Hence, if there is any problem which confronts us at this moment we should face it immediately. That which we set in motion today becomes the experience of tomorrow. But it can never become a fact in our experience unless we first take the specific and definite steps to start it on its way. The future is merely the lengthened shadow of today. It is one with today. It is born out of today. The bright and happy tomorrows of which we dream must not be thought of as something which is about to take place, but must become a mental acceptance as happening *now* as part of our experience.

We have been told that when we pray we must believe that we already possess what we are praying for. This is a definite statement of the Law of Cause and Effect, and most certainly is a scientific approach to demonstration.

Therefore, say to yourself, quietly and with deep conviction:
    I am aware that the power of the Spirit is available to me for every good use I wish to make of It. Recognizing the unity of God and man, I can

desire nothing opposed to the good of the whole, for the hurt of another is my hurt. I know that there is a limitless abundance of good available in the universe, and I now quietly, definitely, and expectantly announce my need and accept its fulfillment.

I know that there is no problem which faces me which is a problem from the standpoint of all-knowing, all-intelligent Spirit. I therefore declare that the answer to my so-called problem is made known when and where it needs to be in order that complete and definite good may come to me. This I accept as my experience, now. And so it is.

CHAPTER XII

SPIRITUAL HEALING

There is too much misunderstanding about spiritual mind healing and the average person does not grasp its full meaning. Spiritual mind healing is not a vague, mystical, mental performance in which one wraps himself with soberness or ponderosity and calls it thinking. Spiritual mind healing is based on the theory that there is an intelligent and creative Power around us and flowing through us; a Power greater than we are but a Power which we can use. At the same time it is a Power that must be consciously used if It is to do anything definite for us. It is like electricity. The universe is full of electrical energy. Machinery is run by this energy, but not a wheel will be turned by it unless it is first properly connected.

Spiritual mind treatment, then, deals with a Power greater than we are and a Power right where we are, around and within us. We cannot change this Power. It exists from eternity to eternity. We might liken It to gravitational force on the surface of this Earth, which automatically holds everything in place, but the force of itself does not change the position of things. We have the freedom to walk about in the gravitational field, to change our position in it. We can stand on our heads or our feet — and gravitational force will never ask, "Are you a Methodist or a Baptist?" or "Are you educated or uneducated? Are you cultured or crude?" It holds everything in its place. Gravitational force is intelligent, it is a power greater than we are that operates upon us and through us.

There is in the universe that which we can call infinite Intelligence and a creative Law surrounding all things, flowing through all things, which in Its original state permeates and penetrates the interspaces of the universe and every object we see.

Someone will ask, "Is that God?"

It is God in the same sense that everything is God. It is God in the same sense that our minds are God. It is God in the sense that God, as the creative Cause of all things, is in and through everything and surrounds everything.

One of the mistakes we make is to think that if we say, "I believe in God, God is Good, God is the only Power there is, God is right where I am," this is a spiritual mind treatment. This is a statement of conviction but not a creative prayer. We do believe that God is all there is, that God is right where we are and what we are. But we should not confuse a statement of our belief with a spiritual mind treatment which is a definite and active thing. Treatment is the activity of our consciousness, our awareness, based on a belief in the Divine Presence, used for a specific purpose, and identified with the purpose, place, or thing we wish to help, to change, or to heal.

A spiritual mind treatment must not be confused with meditation. However, meditation is a good preparation for treatment or prayer. For instance, we might meditate upon the thought: "God is love, God is life, God is truth, God is beauty, God is power," until we feel the presence of life and truth and beauty and power. This increases our awareness of life, love, beauty, and power — and that is good. But if it is to be a treatment, then there must be

75

added to it: "This life, this truth, this love, this beauty, this power is now consciously active in my affairs," or "is eliminating from me what does not belong," or "is establishing in me a poise, a calm, a sense of peace, a sense of belonging, a feeling which is free from fear." In this manner we are passing from the contemplation of the meaning of words, the meditating upon that meaning— all of which is good and essential — to the active application of our words to a specific problem.

For a moment let us consider the act of prayer. It is the finite reaching out to the Infinite for help. It may take the form of supplication or active faith according to our state of consciousness. But when the prayer passes from supplication to active faith, what happens to the mind or the thinking of the one engaged in prayer? The change that takes place is from the idea of "God, please do this," to "Thank you, God, that you are doing this," or "that this is being done." Then we discover that the reaction in the mind of the one praying in this manner is that he accepts his own statement; he passes from hope to faith, to conviction and acceptance. This is called a prayer of affirmation. It is a prayer of acceptance; it is the effective prayer. Whenever one has prayed effectually it has always been because somewhere in the prayer the mind of the one praying has become convinced! The effective prayer is one that has so much faith that the one praying no longer doubts!

It is evident that this must be true because we have to convince either ourselves or God. Now, it stands to reason we cannot tell electricity to be energy, we cannot tell gravitational force to hold things in their places. We can only use the energy and change our position in relation to it. Neither can we tell God anything. As Whittier said: "The Lord is God! He needeth not the poor device of man." It is evident that we cannot argue with the Almighty and tell Him to be good, tell Him to be life, to be truth, beauty, or power. We may only accept that there is a Power greater than we are and that It is operating this way. We must recognize that people who have prayed with fervor and with faith have had their prayers answered. But they were not answered by a caprice of nature, a whimsical fancy of the Almighty, or by some law which is a law of chance in that it might or might not answer. Prayers have always been answered because, knowingly or unknowingly, they have complied with the condition Jesus laid down when he said that when you pray believe that you have received and you will receive.

Jesus introduced the use of a principle that no one had ever heard of before. No one before his time had ever announced such a principle or ever given such a technique. And his teaching was overlooked until the last hundred years, but it now is the foundation of modern metaphysics. What was it Jesus announced? He said, in effect, there is a creative Intelligence surrounding us that operates on our word. Let us add, It operates on our word as gravitational force operates upon an object to hold it where we set it. It operates upon our word as a creative Intelligence operates on a seed that we put into the ground. We do not coerce It, we do not beseech It, we do not supplicate It, we cannot concentrate It; we do not hold thoughts in It, will It, or send thoughts out to influence things, people, or conditions. Instead, It is a Principle, acting as a principle, and therefore acting mathematically and impersonally as all principles must.

Someone might ask, "Is this manipulating God?"

Not at all. This Principle is a law in nature just like other principles. But it is a creative one.

Someone else might ask, "Well, is this merely a mental science? Where is the spiritual value?"

The answer to this is: This Principle reacts to us at the level of our action in It. What It does for us, It must do through us at the level of our conviction, belief, and thought.

If this Power seems to have reacted chaotically it is because our consciousness has been chaotic. Therefore, the spiritual quality of a treatment or prayer is of vital importance. We must not only be aware of the Power, we must tune the mind to a spiritual realization of Life — the embodiment of beauty, of love, of tenderness, of kindness, of compassion, of goodness and faith.

It is impossible, then, to divorce the spiritual conscious-ness from prayer or treatment. The primary step in spiritual mind treatment is an awareness of God. The person who gets the best results is the one who has the most complete conviction of the Divine Presence, and the deepest con-sciousness of spiritual harmony. The treatment must embody that inspiration, that feeling which comes alone from the Source of all life. The treatment must touch the seamless robe of unity and wholeness with conviction and feeling. The higher the spiritual awareness, the more Power will flow through it.

There is a part of us that dwells eternally with the Most High. We cannot divorce spiritual aspiration, spiritual realization, or meditation from a scientific technique. It is still necessary to use the technique. Therefore, at any given moment, if we watch ourselves carefully, we will see that the effectiveness of our treatment will depend on how much of an embodiment there was of love, of compassion, of life, of what I choose to call the abandonment of the mind and the soul to the Spirit. This is not something chaotic. It is something actual and real. It is the acceptance of the availability of the Power greater than we are.

Therefore, say to yourself, quietly and with deep conviction:

I am now waiting upon the Spirit within me. I believe that I am intimately associated with this Spirit. I believe that I am so close to It that It can reach out through me and govern my life in harmony and in peace. I believe It can be a blessing to myself and to others.

I am lifting up my mind, in faith, to the conviction that the Spirit of God within me is my real self. I am inviting this Spirit to enter my mind, to direct my thoughts and my acts, and I am expecting It to do this.

Believing that I am an individual in God and a Divine person in my own right, I am inviting new circumstances and situations into my experience and I am waiting on the Divine Presence within me to make Itself known, to reveal Itself to every person I meet and every situation I contact, to bring life, joy, and happiness to everyone. And so it is.

CHAPTER XIII

HELPING OTHERS

In a spiritual mind treatment we make use of that Power greater than we are by feeling, by conviction, by acceptance, by some Divine sense that everybody has but which few people use. Everybody has it, no one can be without it for God is everywhere and in everything.

Now, let us see how we may use this Divine Power. Suppose John Smith has asked our help and said, "I am very much of a failure in life. Nothing that I do succeeds, nothing works out for me."

We now assume the role of a practitioner and give him a spiritual mind treatment. A treatment is a very definite thing. We do not say, "God bless Johnny. He's a nice boy. And don't forget wife Mary and the children." That is all very sweet, but it is not a treatment. What we say is, "There is only One Power in the universe, that is God. There is only One Actor, that is God. There is only One Movement, which is the movement of God. God is not a failure. God is the very essence of success. John Smith lives and moves and has his being in God."

Continuing our treatment, we say, "John Smith now knows what to do. Divine Intelligence within him tells him what to do. He is now receiving thoughts and ideas and he is impelled to act upon them. He is intelligently guided. John Smith, living in God, is confronted with limitless opportunity for self-expression. Every person he should meet, he will meet; any information he should receive, he will receive. Everything he ought to do, he will do. New situations, new ways of doing things are coming to him." We say this quietly to ourselves, accepting that it is now being done and give thanks that out of the spiritual awareness we have generated our word is manifest in the life of John Smith.

Once a treatment is given it is independent of the one who has given it. We must loose it and let it go. Even though we treat a person once a day, or twice a day, or as often as we wish, our treatment is now acted upon by a Law greater than we are, and it is independent of us. Let me prove this theory by an illustration. If someone were to plant a rosebush in my garden and leave it, it will grow. It is independent of that person; he merely planted it. The Bible says that Paul planted, Apollos watered, but God gave the increase. We must feel that the treatment is independent of us or we will always be sitting around wondering if it is working. We need a conviction beyond faith. The Law cannot do other than respond by corresponding to this conviction.

A treatment is an active statement expressed inaudibly as thinking or audibly as words; it does not matter which so long as it is definite. The treatment is for the purpose of convincing the one giving it, and it operates at whatever level of awareness one reaches during that particular treatment. At times we have a greater level of awareness than at others, but the treatment is always an affirmation of our inner conviction.

There must be faith and conviction and acceptance through the treatment. Here is where our consciousness, having attached itself to a greater possibility, must not limit what *may* happen by what *has* happened. That time track is past. ". . . let the dead bury their dead." Something new and dynamic is being born, right now. The Law, acting on the treatment, is bringing new situations, new people, new ideas, and new activities; It cannot fail to operate at the level of our consciousness.

It might be asked about John, the one whom we are treating, "Can he be helped unless he also believes?"

If we cannot help a person unless he also believes, we will not be able to help many people. His belief has nothing to do with it. It is our belief that has to be transcended, and the transcendence of our belief will neutralize the negativity of his, and do it right where we are and in such degree as the activity of our affirmation takes place at a high level; not the level of concentration, for there is nothing to concentrate. We do not concentrate mathematics. Everybody can add two and two to make four ad infinitum, and never wear out the figure two or exhaust the principle of mathematics which will never even know it has been used. It will always operate automatically and mechanically. So, we have to articulate the treatment and identify it with the one we wish to help. The Law of Mind then automatically and mechanically operates on it at the level of our spiritual awareness.

In treatment we may have to deny something, and we should not be afraid of it. An affirmation and a denial are the same thing because the human mind can only affirm, but it can do so positively or negatively. So we should not worry whether we are affirming or denying. We are arguing to convince ourselves that God is all there is, that there is a Power greater than we are operating right where we are; all the confusion of thought or ignorance of this truth cannot change one bit of it. When we use a principle there is no whimsical response either of the Almighty or the less mighty. It is an absolute Law of action and reaction activated by consciousness, and a high degree of awareness inevitably produces a greater reaction.

Suppose Mary Jones has some kind of physical difficulty and we are going to treat her for physical perfection. We start: "God is Perfect. Mary is a creation of God and is living in a spiritual universe now. Her body is not separate from the Essence and Perfection of Reality. It is perfect, there is only right action; there is no inaction or wrong action, no overaction or underaction. This word is a law of elimination to everything that does not belong to her. Mary's body now manifests its natural rhythm and harmony because it is now tuned in to That which is the very essence of rhythm and harmony and love. Perfect love casts out all fear; therefore, there is no longer any fear in her and she has an inward consciousness, an awareness, of life and action and wholeness. There is no condemnation in God. Mary Jones now knows that she is one with God, with the universe, and with people. She has no feeling of rejection, she has no sense of guilt, she loves, is loving, and is loved. There is a radiant happiness, there is a dynamic vitality, there is an enthusiastic zest for life. Everything responds to this. Her body is a body of perfect ideas. There is perfect assimilation, perfect circulation, and perfect elimination. I accept the manifestation of these ideas in her experience, right now. And so it is."

All this we must *feel*. We are not sending out anything, holding anything, or concentrating anything; we are not supplicating anything, willing anything, or wishing. *We are stating and knowing the nature of spiritual Reality.* This is a spiritual mind treatment.

Spiritual awareness will make us all better, giving us a tranquillity, happiness, and sense of well-being, so that we shall no longer be afraid of the universe, or of the past, present, or future. Knowing this can heal. The Bible says that the invisible things of God are made manifest through the visible. Our word is the Law in action. It is the motivation of It.

Effective prayer gives definite proof that God is an active

agent in His own creation and that it is given to man to use the Agency of that creation lovingly, justly, and kindly; dispassionately, in a sense, because It is a Law, but with certainty of getting a result. Our own lives may impart to their environment something which enabled the woman by touching the seamless garment to be made whole, and the words of our mouth speak forth some teaching which others may use. And down the pathway of our experience again shall the deaf hear, the blind see, the lame walk; and those who suffer from fear and stupification and intoxication of the race mind in which we are immersed shall arise and sing.

CHAPTER XIV

SELF-AWARENESS

Nature made a chemical laboratory within us to take care of our health. In a sense we might say that there are little intelligences within us acting as though they were little people, whose business it is to digest our food and assimilate it, to circulate our blood and get rid of its impurities. There are millions of these little people inside our bodies whose purpose it is to keep us physically fit. But there also are other little people who are not so kindly minded and they try to tear things down and disrupt the work of the good little people.

Every doctor knows that when he can get the good people inside working with him, things are going to come out all right. We break a bone and when it is set nature gets busy and all the good little people begin to knit the bone together again, and all the time they are causing the blood to circulate so there will be no infection.

One of the most popular psychologists in America told me that he once suffered from indigestion and the thought came to him that he could talk to these little people inside him and tell them that it really was their business to take care of his digestion. So he talked to them for a few moments every day and told them how wonderful they were and how much he appreciated what they were doing and that he wasn't going to interfere with them any more. He was going to be happy and he knew they would take care of everything for him. He praised them and blessed them, and in a few weeks his physical condition cleared up.

Well, this is a body-mind relationship. It is reducing psychosomatics to its simplest common denominator. There is an Intelligence hid at the center of everything and we are intelligent and the lower form of intelligence responds to the higher form. The intelligence in the physical body is a subconscious intelligence. It works creatively, but within certain fixed limitations. It is like a man sent on an errand and told what to do and knowing only to do what he is told.

But we are learning that we can interfere with the good little people inside us because they are subject to a greater intelligence than theirs, which is the person himself. They are supposed to be working for us and with us, but we can so disturb them that they work destructively instead of constructively.

This can be carried to such an extent that the wrong direction given to these little people produces a large part of our physical diseases. But right direction can reverse this process and produce physical well-being instead of disease. And we now know that while hate, animosity, and confusion can produce discord, love can heal it.

It is helpful to imagine and feel that all the little people inside that are working for us and with us are connected with the Divine Intelligence which directs them — the very Power that created them. This brings us back to the need that we all have for a faith, a calm assurance, and an inward sense of well-being.

Not only is there an Intelligence directing the activities of our physical bodies, this same Intelligence is also directing everything we do. Not only does man operate against himself, physically, he does so in every activity of his life. How many of us really expect to be happy tomorrow? How many of us, when we lie down at night, relax and let the bed hold us up? How many of us have confidence enough in God to sleep in peace, wake in joy, and look forward to the coming day with gladness?

What we need is a conscious cooperation, and a glad one, between ourselves and the Power which, if we let It, would rightly govern everything. But man is so used to operating against himself, so used to thinking of himself as detached and separate, he has so completely taken the whole burden of life on his own shoulders, that he has almost lost the ability to cooperate with that Divine Presence which seeks to be a partner to all of us. In our ignorance we have not only operated against ourselves, we have contradicted the supremacy of God. We have denied ourselves the privilege of working with rather than against the Power that put us here.

We know that we did not set the stars in their courses; we did not cause the sun to shine or the rain to come; however, we can cooperate with this Power back of us. But we cannot unify and cooperate with something we do not believe in. So the starting point, the very beginning of the reeducation of our minds, must be a deep conviction, a firm faith. And since, in a sense, life is a stage on which each plays a part, there is no reason why we should not dramatize our relationship with the Infinite.

Just think of all these little people working inside us! God put them there. Why not hook them up in our imagination with the living Spirit and recognize their presence, praise and bless them, and even tell them what we want them to do. And each day think how wonderful it is to be cooperating with God! Surely this is the greatest drama of all.

But we must not forget the Director of the play, the One who knows how to make each separate line and act become part of the whole piece until something complete is produced. God is the Great Producer, the Great Director, and the One who knows all the parts and where each one belongs. And we must learn to believe in this Producer and Director, even though He is invisible. We cannot see the little people inside us but they are there, and in our imagination we can sense them.

Therefore, say to yourself, quietly and with deep conviction:

My body is the temple of the living Spirit. It is spiritual substance now. Every part of my body is in harmony with the living Spirit within me. The Life of this Spirit flows through every atom of my being, vitalizing, invigorating, and renewing every part of my physical body.

There is a pattern of perfection at the center of my being which is now operating through every organ, function, action, and reaction. My body is forever renewed by the Spirit and I am now made vigorous and whole.

The Life of the Spirit is my life, and Its strength is my strength. I am born of the Spirit. I am in the Spirit. I am the Spirit made manifest. And so it is.

CHAPTER XV

THE ETERNAL NOW

One of the questions so frequently asked me is, "Do you believe in immortality, and do you believe that all people are immortal?" Personally, I consider that the immortality of the individual life has been conclusively proved; and I am convinced that you and I and everyone else are destined to live forever, because the life which we now experience is the Life of God in us. It is this Life of God in us that is eternal, not the external form of flesh.

In a certain sense, each one of us is two persons. One is physical and the other is mental or spiritual. The mental or spiritual uses a physical body in this world because it needs it. But at the time of death the spirit within us, which is independent of this physical form, severs itself from it, or as the Bible says: "Or ever the silver cord be loosed . . . . Then shall the dust return to the earth as it was: and the spirit shall return unto God who gave it."

To those who have inward vision, it is not at all uncommon to see the separation of the spirit from the body. And perhaps more frequently than we have realized, after this separation takes place we are able to communicate with those who have left this world. Personally, I have not the slightest doubt of this because I have had too many experiences in this field to question its reality. It has been my privilege to know a number of highly trained scientists who have spent years of very careful research into this subject only to come to the conclusion that there is an immortal side to our nature. There is something about the personality that does not die, that continues beyond the grave.

But someone might ask, "How can you believe this when you are dealing with such an intangible thing? How can you trust your feelings and sentiments alone? Perhaps the whole thing is but an idle daydream, an empty wish, a forlorn hope?"

You might as well ask an artist if his vision of beauty is a forlorn hope. He does not see the beauty but he does feel it. You might as well ask a mathematician whether or not the principle of mathematics is a reality. No one has ever weighed or measured it.

As a matter of fact, while biology is the study of the Life Principle in the physical body, no one has ever seen this Life Principle. And yet, at the very moment that it departs from the body, the body begins to disintegrate. Who can doubt that the integrating factor, the thing that held the body together, has actually left its earthly home?

Psychology is the science of the way the mind works in us; but no psychologist ever saw the mind, nor is there one who doubts its existence. It is an interesting fact but a true one, that all we deal with in this physical world is the effect of invisible causes, of an invisible Intelligence working through physical forms.

Jesus said: "In my Father's house are many mansions: if it were not so, I would have told you." In other words, there are different planes of existence and we progress from one to the other, always more and never less ourselves. We can see how this principle works right here in this world. There is a certain form of intelligence even in a piece of steel. There is an atomic intelligence in every physical object. And then we see another level or gradation of this intelligence in animal life. Then it broadens out and reaches the human being, and we find this same intelligence with conscious awareness.

Next, we find that occasionally some people have what is called cosmic intelligence, which takes in a lot more territory. We speak of them as being illumined and spiritually aware. Jesus, of course, was the greatest of these, and he definitely said that he knew about this world and about the next one. He knew how people lived here and how they lived there.

Everything that Jesus did was done as an object lesson to teach us the relationship we have to this world, to each other, to the next world, and to God. He taught that there is no long period between sleeping to this world and waking to the next; for he said to the thief on the cross beside him: "Verily I say unto thee, To day shalt thou be with me in paradise." It seems as though the whole life and teaching of Jesus was to give people the hope and the assurance not only that they are one with God, but also that their personal lives will continue to exist beyond the grave.

There is no doubt that he had spiritual power enough at his command to resist any violence had he so wished. In order to teach the lesson that he wanted us all to learn, it was necessary that he permit himself to be crucified, that his body be placed in a tomb, and that he become resurrected and appear as he did to hundreds of people who knew him personally so that there would no longer be any doubt in their minds.

The triumph of the cross was infinitely more than one man proving that he was immortal. It was a lesson, chosen for a definite purpose. The cross stands for the Tree of Life whose roots are in the earth, whose arms or branches are stretched out in a protective manner, and whose head or top-piece is pointed toward the sky. This really represents the threefold nature of man — spiritual, mental, and physical:

or, as the Bible says, spirit, soul, and body. And so Jesus permitted that which was human about him to hang on this Tree of Life and to be taken down and placed in a tomb, which stands for everything that means obstruction to life, everything that looks as though life were buried, inactive, and dead.

Let us not forget that even in this experience the tomb was filled with a Light — the Light that the Bible says lighteth every man's pathway, the eternal Light of heaven. And it was this Light, this Life, that Jesus took into the tomb with him. It was this Light that emerged from the tomb. The cross and the suffering and the anguish and the tomb were but preliminary incidents to the resurrection, to the triumph of the spirit; and the certainty that the cross cannot long crucify nor the tomb long contain that which is destined to live forever.

It is no wonder that the Psalmist long ago chanted: "Whither shall I go from thy spirit? or whither shall I flee from thy presence? If I ascend up into heaven, thou art there: if I make my bed in hell, behold, thou art there. If I take the wings of the morning, and dwell in the uttermost parts of the sea; Even there shall thy hand lead me, and thy right hand shall hold me. If I say, Surely the darkness shall cover me; even the night shall be light about me." Again in a great psalm of confidence he says: "Yea, though I walk through the valley of the shadow of death, I will fear no evil: for thou art with me; thy rod and thy staff they comfort me." We might call these the songs of the boundless soul, hymns of praise to the eternal Creator; a glad and joyful recognition that that life which has been given to man is guided and guarded into eternal pathways of self-expansion.

But perhaps there is more than one cross from which we need to be delivered; more than one tomb that needs to be opened. Fear and lack, failure, disease, and unhappiness are crosses upon which we hang until the day of deliverance.

And too often we lie in some tomb of uncertainty and deny our good. However, even here there is a Light accompanying us. Even here there is a Voice that still speaks, telling us that the tomb does not really represent life, that we can arise and walk forth free and whole.

What we need to do, then, is to rediscover the secret that Jesus knew, which carried him triumphantly through every experience of life and finally delivered him from the last enemy of man — death. He gave us the key when he said: "I and my Father are one." " . . . the words that I speak unto you I speak not of myself: but the Father that dwelleth in me, he doeth the works." " . . . for my Father is greater than I. "

It was this understanding that God is all there is which gave Jesus the power to do everything he did, whether it was the miracles of healing or the raising of himself from the dead. I believe the possibility of all these things rests on just one simple proposition: There is One Life, that Life is God, and that Life is every man's life.

Of course, we are human beings and we do miss our friends. But when we understand that every man is immortal, that death is but the gateway to a larger life, we shall have a different viewpoint; and often, indeed, we shall recognize that our loss is their gain. It is necessary for us to realize that immortality is a principle in nature and comes alike to everyone. Sanity would forbid us to believe that some persons are immortal and others are not.

Jesus understood this and that is why he said that God causes His sun and rain to come alike on the just and the unjust. He knew that for the most part man does not live as though he were an eternal being; that he gets caught up with his little problems and often gets lost in the maze of his own confusion. But he saw through all this to the final end of man. He knew that every person has the same Divine spark within him; that finally the Spirit will triumph in everyone's life; and that good comes to all.

But he also said that the good is here now could we but see it; that the Kingdom of God is at hand and we need to realize it. And he told about a daily resurrection that we may experience. We already possess the power, and when we no longer carry the burdens of yesterday into our tomorrows, we shall find each day a day of resurrection and rejoicing. Immortality is something to be experienced here and now. Each person can open his mind to that other side of himself, that part which seems never to have been completely caught in the flesh.

We do not earn our immorality. It is a gift of God. But we do have to earn the ability to experience and enjoy it. This is a gift we shall have to make to ourselves. This world and the next are but two parts of one journey, which can, if we permit it, be filled with hope and joy.

Therefore, say to yourself, quietly and with deep conviction:

Today I am entering on a new life. The doorway of opportunity is open wide before me. There is something within me that is alert and aware. My will, my thought, my imagination, feel and sense new opportunities for self-expression. I identify myself with success. I am one with it. New ideas are coming to me, new ways of doing things.

I have complete confidence that I shall recognize the opportunity when it presents itself; that I shall know what to do under every circumstance and in every situation. There is a deep feeling within me that all is well. I am ready and willing to give of the best I have to life, and I know that the best that life has will come back to me.

Believing that all the power there is is back of every constructive thought; believing that I live in a Divine Presence which flows through everything; believing that I am guided by an infinite

Intelligence which knows everything, I live this day in complete assurance, I live this day in complete happiness. And I expect that every tomorrow will be an increasing unfoldment, an increasing revelation of that good which is eternally available for every person who lives. And so it is.